# GREAT LIVES OBSERVED

Gerald Emanuel Stearn, *General Editor*

EACH VOLUME IN THE SERIES VIEWS THE CHARACTER AND ACHIEVEMENT OF A GREAT WORLD FIGURE IN THREE PERSPECTIVES—THROUGH HIS OWN WORDS, THROUGH THE OPINIONS OF HIS CONTEMPORARIES, AND THROUGH RETROSPECTIVE JUDGMENTS—THUS COMBINING THE INTIMACY OF AUTOBIOGRAPHY, THE IMMEDIACY OF EYEWITNESS OBSERVATION, AND THE OBJECTIVITY OF MODERN SCHOLARSHIP

JEROME CH'EN, *the editor of this volume in the Great Lives Observed series, is Senior Lecturer at the School of History, University of Leeds, England. He received his M.A. degree from the Nankai Institute of Economics, in China, and his Ph.D. from the University of London. Dr. Ch'en is also the author of* Mao and the Chinese Revolution *and* Yuan Shih-k'ai: Brutus Assumes the Purple. *He is the translator of a book of medieval Chinese poems,* Poems of Solitude, *and has written numerous articles and reviews.*

GREAT LIVES OBSERVED

# MAO

## Edited by JEROME CH'EN

*What makes him formidable is that he is not
just a Party boss but by millions of Chinese
is quite genuinely regarded as a teacher,
statesman, strategist, philosopher, poet laureate,
national hero, head of the family,
and the greatest liberator in history.*

—EDGAR SNOW

A SPECTRUM BOOK

PRENTICE-HALL, INC., ENGLEWOOD CLIFFS, N.J.

All translations in this book are by
the editor, unless otherwise indicated.

# Acknowledgements

The editor of this anthology wishes to express his deepest thanks to all his friends and colleagues who have kindly helped him in its compilation and, in particular, Mr. Edgar Snow and Professor Takeuchi Minoru for their generous permission to use their writings.

He is also immensely grateful for permission to use the publications of the *Asahi Shimbun* of Tokyo, the Monitoring Department of the British Broadcasting Corporation of Reading, the *China Quarterly* of London, Columbia University Press of New York, Editions Gallimard of Paris, Grove Press of New York, Hamish Hamilton of London, Harvard University Press of Cambridge, Mass., Holt, Rinehart & Winston, Inc., of New York, Oxford University Press of London, Pall Mall Press of London, Penguin Books of Middlesex, Frederick A. Praeger, Inc., of New York, Random House, Inc., of New York, the *Sekai Shuho* of Tokyo and the *Survey* of London.

# Contents

GREAT LIVES OBSERVED

# MAO

# Introduction

'The Cultural Revolution has made it necessary for all students of the Chinese Communist movement and of Mao's role in it to take stock once again. The structural changes in both the Chinese state and the Chinese Party in the midst of this great convulsion are now seen to stem from deep historical roots. These, however, have been revealed only recently and now require fresh interpretations. The Cultural Revolution certainly bears the stamp of Mao's style of thinking and of campaigning, but it also has vented his anti-elitist and voluntarist traits with unprecedented intensity. This short essay is not designed to cover all aspects of Mao's long and notable career; for a comprehensive account of it, readers are recommended to consult the several excellent studies available to them. What may be attempted here is to trace and analyze the historical development of the crucial triangular relationship between Mao, the Chinese Communist Party (CCP), and the Chinese masses.

The elusive concept of Mao's style must be used with care. What is meant here are several recurrent themes persistently characterizing his thought and action from his youth through to the present. To understand these themes, which spring from the character of the man himself, it is necessary to begin with a brief discussion of the cultural and political background of his formative years in his native province, Hunan, which he did not leave until he was almost 25 years old. The extent to which the particularistic traditions of the province marked a man of Mao's generation in China may be imagined when one realizes that communications media on a national scale were almost entirely lacking. There was scarcely any national consensus to speak of, but only strong provincial attitudes toward cultural and political matters. It is to his Hunanese environment, therefore, that some of his early ideas may be traced. These ideas, together with others, were to typify that "Chineseness" so often referred to as regards his later "sinocization" of Marxism-Leninism.

1

During the eighteenth and early nineteenth centuries, the scholars of Hunan distinguished themselves for their pragmatic and interpretative approach to the Confucian texts, which at that time constituted the main body of all Chinese learning. By constantly stressing the political and economic significance of these studies, Hunanese work contrasted sharply with the scholasticism dominant elsewhere in China. Cultural insulation was partly responsible for this. For instance, none of the great eighteenth-century masters of classics and history ever had visited Hunan in the capacity of either a visiting lecturer or an examiner. There was also Hunan's own academic tradition, beginning with the pragmatism of Wang Fu-chih (1619–1692), an anti-Manchu philosopher of Hengyang who discoursed on a vast variety of subjects. He was subsequently admired generation after generation in his native province. Contrary to the prevalent dogma that the Golden Age had existed only in the past and hence a reversion to the past meant an improvement upon the present, Wang expounded an evolutionary view of political institutions: since each historical period had its own adequate political organization, it was futile to revive an archaic form of polity.

> Imperial succession through courteous abdication [as from Yao to Shun] was unknown in primeval times; righteous uprisings against a guilty regime [as Shang against Hsia] were unknown in the times of Yao and Shun; the present arrangement was unknown in the Han and T'ang dynasties; and what will be the arrangement in future is still unknown today.[1]

Political and social systems, in his view, were alterable; so were human nature and social customs. The former, to be sure, had to adapt themselves to suit the latter. Of the latter, said Wang, "when a [new] custom is established, human nature is re-shaped in the process." He went on: "What is not yet complete can be completed; what is already completed can be reformed. There is not a single part of human nature already shaped that cannot be modified." [2]

Change, in Wang's scheme, knew almost no limit, and changes in man and his institutions were continuous in history. As to learn-

---

[1] Wang Fu-chih, *Chou-i wai-chuan*, chüan, 5.

[2] Wang Fu-chih, *Shang-shu yin-i, t'ai-chia*, chüan, 2.

ing and knowledge, he preferred the dual approach of observation and deduction.

> Observe natural phenomena extensively and investigate the events of the past and present so as to establish [them] beyond any doubt. This is what is meant by *ke-wu* (investigation of things). Then generalize in order to throw light on them and think in order to exhaust all their hidden meanings. This is what is meant by *chih-chih* (achievement of knowledge). Without the process of deduction, things remain unassessed and tend to corrupt us and befog our sense of direction; without the process of observation and investigation, knowledge is useless and tends to lead us into heresy. When both methods complement each other, there is no chance of their going astray.[3]

Practical observation and abstract thinking thus received equal emphasis in Wang's process of knowing. But he went a step further, to make a significant distinction between knowledge and action: "Action can reap the result of knowledge whereas knowledge may not lead to action." [4]

The interpretative (rather than textual) and pragmatic (rather than metaphysical) traditions of the Hunan school of Confucianism characterized the responses of the scholars of that province after the Opium War of 1839–42. Ho Ch'ang-ling (1785–1848) earlier had compiled the popular and influential anthology of political and economic essays of the Ch'ing dynasty (first published in 1827). Wei Yuan (1794–1857), his friend and colleague, who had served under the redoubtable Commissioner Lin Tse-hsü, published his treatise on world history and geography, the *Hai-kuo t'u-chih* (1844), whose impact on nineteenth-century China and Japan hardly could be exaggerated. Through like-mindedness or personal ties, often both, these and other scholars of Hunan established close connections with such pillars of state of the 1860's and 1870's as Tseng Kuo-fan, Tso Tsung-t'ang, and Hu Lin-i, all belonging to the same pragmatic school of Confucianism and all being Hunanese. From 1850 onward, when rebellions swept across most of the empire, Hunan alone provided great leaders who could deal with the crises.

[3] Wang Fu-chih, *Shuo-ming, chung*, chüan, 2.
[4] Wang Fu-chih, *Shuo-ming, chung*, chüan, 2.

The explanation behind this characteristic response lies partly in the special qualities of the Hunan elite.

From 1889 to 1907, the powerful and learned viceroy of Hupei and Hunan was Chang Chih-tung (1837–1909), a pragmatic Confucian. In the years after the traumatic event of China's defeat by Japan in 1895, he was instrumental in the appointment of men of a modernist bent, such as Ch'en Pao-chen, Huang Tsun-hsien, and Chiang Piao, to posts of consequence in Hunan. Through them, the province led the empire in adopting reformist measures—for instance, the introduction of modern schools and modern industries. Mineral resources, for which Hunan is famous, were opened up, and a railroad was projected that would link up Wuhan and Canton by cutting right across the province. At the initiative of these officials —Ch'en the governor, Huang the censor, and Chiang the commissioner for education—native radicals like T'an Ssu-t'ung (an admirer of Wang Fu-chih and Wei Yuan) and outside progressives like Liang Ch'i-ch'ao were given opportunities, and encouragement, to impart their views to students and the public in Hunan. T'an also inspired his fellow provincials with action such as the organization of the patriotic Southern Study Society, the publication of a periodical called *Hsiang Pao*, and eventually his martyrdom in the Reform of 1898.[5]

The failure of the Reform drove many intellectuals to accept revolution as the inevitable road to China's salvation. This reorientation affected a younger generation of Hunan elite—e.g., Huang Hsing, Sung Chiao-jen, and Ch'en T'ien-hua. Reform might conceivably be carried out by intellectuals alone; revolution needed allies and a popular base. T'an Ssu-t'ung already had shown an appreciation of the strength of the secret societies; the new elite growing up after him did not hesitate to make direct appeal to them. These societies, drawing their membership largely from the lower classes, had been instrumental in the overthrow of the dynasties in the past and were mostly anti-Manchu in an active or in a passive sense. Being less sophisticated than the educated elite, they saw political changes mainly as violent action. In normal times, therefore,

[5] *Hunan chin-pai-nien ta-shih chi-shu* [An account of the important events in Hunan in the last hundred years] (Ch'angsha, 1959), pp. 147–49, 157–58.

no political consensus existed between them and the gentry, but when a crisis loomed, a convergence of views was not impossible.

The ideological preparation for such a convergence at the beginning of this century was laid by the revival of the myth that the Han-Chinese, the majority of the nation living under the Manchu rule, were the descendants of the Yellow Emperor, hence ethnically superior to the Manchus. It was believed that by a racial revolution aiming at the overthrow of the regime of an inferior race, the Han-Chinese would be able, when in power, to put the country in better order and lead it to power and wealth. In an age of introspective nationalism and social Darwinism, this racial substitution in governing the country presented to the Chinese their only hope for international equality and national independence.

The predominant secret society in Hunan at the time of the T'aip'ing Rebellion (1850–1864) was the Heaven-Earth Society. The Society, antagonistic to the Manchus, staged simultaneous uprisings when the T'aip'ing invaded Hunan. However, due to a lack of cooperation between the various rebels, the uprisings ended in failure. In 1856, when the last of the uprisings led by it was quelled, the Society's influence in the province was eradicated. The social vacuum thus created was filled by a politically more moderate society, the Elder Brothers, most of whose members came from the ranks of the local militia and Tseng Kuo-fan and Tso Tsung-t'ang's Hunan army. Without this society to take over the social and economic functions of the now disintegrated Heaven-Earth Society, it would have been difficult to organize the work of rehabilitation and reconstruction, or even to maintain law and order. In 1852, when the T'aip'ing invaded Hunan for the first time, it encountered the Heaven-Earth Society; ten years later, when it invaded the province again, it found the Elder Brothers. Later, in 1900, although the Elder Brothers refrained from supporting the Boxers, their anti-Manchuism furnished fertile ground on which ethnic nationalism could flourish. The intellectuals of Hunan, in transplanting their nationalist views to the secret societies, performed the role of catalysts; reform and revolution thus joined forces.

The 1906 uprising in P'inghsiang, Liuyang, and Liling, though an abortive one, was nevertheless the first tangible result of this conjunction. It declared, "China is the China of the Chinese and the Han-Chinese is the greatest and best race of the world." [6] Such a race should be able, according to the manifesto of the uprising, to create a happy republic based upon the principles of equality and liberty, the equalization of land rights, and the solution of social problems. The scene of the uprising was the stronghold of the Elder Brothers (otherwise known as the Hung Chiang Hui), which was the site of one of China's biggest coal mines. This uprising's alliance of intelligentsia and secret society was to be repeated in the 1911 revolution that finally toppled the Manchu dynasty.

The influence of all these provincial characteristics—pragmatism and interpretativeness, emphasis on both investigation and reasoning, relationship between knowledge and action (theory and practice), reform and revolution, pride in the Han race, and willingness to co-operate with the lower classes (even the choice of the geographic setting of the Autumn Harvest Uprising, P'inghsiang and Liuyang, in 1927)—may be found in Mao's thought and action. To complete the account, two modern trends that Hunan shared with other provinces in the modernization in the first decade of this century should be added: equality between the sexes and enthusiasm for physical education. In 1903, Ch'angsha, the provincial capital, saw the establishment of its first girls' school.[7] During the 1911 revolution, Hunanese women leaders not only demanded equal rights for both sexes and the abolition of arranged marriages, but also formed a league to promote women's participation in politics and even a ladies' contingent to join the proposed northern expedition of the revolutionaries. Ch'angsha then had its first, though short-lived, woman's newspaper, the *Women's Rights*.[8] Another thing that caught the imagination of the Hunanese as well as of many people of other provinces was physical training; this was due to the influence of social Darwinism (the survival of the physically fittest) and of Japan. Huang Hsing, a revolutionary, and Hsiung Hsi-ling, a reformer, for example, had both been physical training teachers

[6] Chug-kuo Shih-hsüeh-hui, ed., *Hsin-hai ke-ming* [The 1911 revolution] (Shanghai, 1957), II, 475–78.

[7] *Hunan chin-pai-nien ta-shih chi-shu*, pp. 196–97.

[8] *Hsin-hai ke-ming hui-i-lu* [Reminiscences of the 1911 revolution] (Peking, 1962), II, 195.

before turning their attention to politics.[9] These developments also made their impression upon the mind of the young Mao.

This was the intellectual and political atmosphere in Hunan on the eve of the 1911 revolution, when Mao, at the age of 17, became interested in political matters. He went to Hsianghsiang, a neighboring town of his native Shaoshan, to attend a primary school, where he was introduced to the writings of the Reformers of 1898— K'ang Yu-wei, Liang Ch'i-ch'ao, and Cheng Kuan-ying. He seems to have been more impressed by their literary persuasiveness than by the cogency of their involved arguments, as can be illustrated by two ensuing events. In the spring of 1911, when he arrived at Ch'angsha, he read the revolutionary organ, the *People's Strength*. It excited him so much that he immediately wrote his first "wall poster," advocating a republican government with Sun Yat-sen as president, K'ang Yu-wei as premier, and Liang Ch'i-ch'ao as foreign secretary.[10] The naïveté of this proposal needs no explanation, for the revolutionary Sun was an irreconcilable opponent of reformist K'ang and Liang.[11] Any idea of co-operation between them was mere wishful thinking. The tide of events in 1911 naturally proved Mao wrong. He joined the revolutionary army, and this action deleted all traces of reformism from his mind.

The First Normal School, to which Mao was admitted soon afterwards, was not an institution for meticulous research. Instead, moral behavior, physical training, and social activities[12] were the tenor of the education Mao received there. Utilitarian though it was, the school failed to evoke his interest in mathematics, natural sciences, and English. His ignorance of natural science is clearly shown later, in his published works;[13] he has scarcely even ventured to use scien-

[9] *Hsin-hai ke-ming hui-i-lu*, II, 112, 133. See also Mao's letter to Miyazaki Toten in 1917 in which Mao expressed his admiration of Huang Hsing. The *Asahi Shimbun*, July 3, 1967.

[10] Hsiao San, *Mao Tse-tung t'ung-chih ti ch'ing-shao-nien shih-tai* [Comrade Mao Tse-tung's boyhood and youth] (Peking, 1949), p. 35. The fact that Hsiao could first publish this story in an article in the *Liberation Daily* [Chieh-fang jih-pao] (Yenan), December 14, 1941, to herald the personality cult of Mao may mean that Mao was then still able to laugh off his juvenile wishful thinking.

[11] Compare this with "A Talk in Hangchow," translated below, pp. 103–4.

[12] Li Jui, *Mao Tse-tung t'ung-chih ti ch'u-ch'i ke-ming huo-tung* [Comrade Mao Tse-tung's early revolutionary activities] (Peking, 1957), p. 18.

[13] See below, "On the Ten Great Relationships," pp. 67–71, and "A Talk in Hangchow," p. 107.

tific metaphors and has maintained a completely voluntarist or activist view of the limitless abilities of man. The little science he did acquire in school was essentially that of the nineteenth century, with its unbounded faith in the total conquest of nature by man. With such a rudimentary understanding of science, Mao wholly accepted the rationalities and irrationalities of Wang Fu-chih's theory of human nature when he came under the influence of Yang Ch'ang-chi, an admirer of Wang (he was to become Mao's father-in-law posthumously) and when he attended the lectures sponsored by the Ch'uan-shan Society (Ch'uan-shan being Wang's courtesy name).[14] His association with the Ch'uan-shan Society, begun before 1918, was to continue until 1920.[15] Wang's view of the malleability of human nature fitted in well with the dynamism of Marx, which Mao embraced later. Thus Mao's understanding of human nature is founded upon Mencius's exposition of the goodness of man, Wang's of man's malleability, the dialectics of Marx, and, above all, his own rich experience in handling men; modern studies of human nature never have formed a part of his scheme. At the time when he became acquainted with Wang Fu-chih's theory, Mao was also interested in questions of morality (his reading of F. Paulsen), philosophy (his notes of reading on the subject), and current affairs (his avid reading of newspapers). Never a painstaking researcher, Mao was likely to have rejected what he considered as the scholasticism of Wang, of Paulsen, and of other writers, while absorbing only the points of practical use. With this mixture of revolutionary, utilitarian, and voluntarist thoughts germinating in his mind, he found the *New Youth*, the radical journal, edited by Ch'en Tu-hsiu, eminently palatable and read it regularly. Having thus prepared himself, he went to Peking in 1918 to place himself under the patronage and influence of Li Ta-chao.

China was never, and still is not, a country with elaborate institutional safeguards against human frailties; her tradition was simply that good administration depended upon good men. For a Chinese politician, therefore, it was more important to have an understand-

---

[14] Li Jui, *op. cit.*, pp. 22–24, and Hsiao San, *Mao Tse-tung t'ung-chih: erh-t'ung shih-tai, ch'ing-nien shih-tai, yü ch'u-ch'i ke-ming huo-tung* [Comrade Mao Tse-tung's boyhood, youth, and early revolutionary activities] (Shantung, 1947), p. 18.

[15] *Chou-mo-pao* [The weekend] (Ch'angsha), I, 3.

ing of men than to have a sound knowledge of the workings of her political and legal systems. With his focus upon men rather than upon institutions, Mao had no prejudice against anarchism. The Chinese government of 1918 being corrupt and inept, Mao's reaction to anarchist propaganda was favorable. But the fascination was only ephemeral. Later in his life, his impatience with bureaucracy and legal formalities sprang perhaps more from his traditional political understanding than from the influence of Kropotkin and Tolstoy.[16]

Li Ta-chao imparted to Mao two of his convictions: (1) a belief in the yet untapped surplus energy of the broad masses, however backward they might be; (2) another belief that the immense potentials of the peasantry of China were still waiting to be exploited.[17] The historical significance of this type of incipient, crude class analysis lay in its supplanting the racial analysis of the 1900's. The belief in the Han-Chinese being superior to the Manchus injected a new self-confidence into the overwhelming majority of the nation and justified their racial revolution. The Han-Chinese rule from 1912 to 1918, however, had fallen sadly short of its original expectations, causing the nation to sink into a morass of dismay. An expression of the consequent inferiority feeling of the Han-Chinese was Lu Hsün's famous image of Ah Q. By a class analysis, the Chinese would be able to divide the sheep from the goats, as it were, and by sacrificing the goats, the nation could purge itself of all sins, so as to revive its hopes for national power and wealth.

From what little is known of his writings in 1919–21, Mao did not yet fully appreciate the significance of a class analysis. For instance, in his "Great Union of the Masses," published in 1919 (the only copy of its full text is in Peking and never has been reproduced in full for circulation), his hopes of the masses as a source of power were still pinned more upon their unity and *numerical* strength than upon their revolutionary *qualities*. The masses had their oppressors, of course, but Mao was not yet quite capable of clearly differentiating these two classes of men. None the less, the essay

[16] Li Jui, *op. cit.*, p. 91 and R. Payne, *Mao Tse-tung, Ruler of Red China* (London, 1950), pp. 55–56.

[17] S. R. Schram, *The Political Thought of Mao Tse-tung* (New York, London, 1963), pp. 17–18 and M. Meisner, *Li Ta-chao and the Origins of Chinese Marxism* (Cambridge, Mass., 1967), pp. 263–64.

showed that its author had a fervent faith in the masses and that he was in the process of giving up the notion of racial superiority for an unconventional notion of class superiority. He was as yet no Marxist.

His transition to Marxism-Leninism came quickly against the background of a rapid spread of Communist propaganda in 1920. In this, Li Ta-chao, Ch'en Tu-hsiu, and especially his friend Ts'ai Ho-sen played their part. From May to September, 1920, Ts'ai wrote to Mao from France, arguing that under the present social system, there was no hope for a solution to any of China's basic problems. Solutions could be found only after the system itself had been changed by a social revolution in which the main forces had to be the "small" workers and peasants.

> Some say that there is no class distinction in China; this I cannot accept. Although the small workers and peasants ignorantly ascribe their poverty and misery to fate, their strength is certainly no less than those in eastern and western Europe once they become class conscious.[18]

The instrument by which the masses could become class conscious was a party that "is the prime mover, instigator, agitator, vanguard, and field headquarters of the revolution. In view of the present situation in China (in two years) such a party should be organized to give the revolution a nerve center." [19] To these views espoused by the ideologically more advanced Ts'ai, Mao could only say: "There is not a single word with which I disagree." [20]

From his conversion to Marxism to his temporary retirement from politics in 1924–25, Mao's activities and views showed a conventional acceptance of the Comintern and of the CCP line and an uncertain grasp of Marxism-Leninism. Urban work, mainly among the workers of P'inghsiang and Liuyang and the intellectuals in Canton and Shanghai cast into relief only his inadequacies. His intellectual standing was far too inferior to that of the contemporary

[18] *Hsin-min-hsüeh-hui hui-yuan t'ung-hsun chi* [Correspondence of the members of the New Citizens' Study Society], No. 3, quoted from *Hunan li-shih tzu-liao* [History material of Hunan], No. 4 (1959), p. 80.

[19] *Hunan li-shih tzu-liao*, No. 4 (1959), p. 81.

[20] Li Jui, *op. cit.*, p. 136.

leaders in the Nationalist Party (KMT) and the CCP. In a circle that paid so much attention to degrees, publications, social position, and academic records,[21] Mao could scarcely hope to rise above a position of secondary importance. The official organs of both parties, for instance, were filled with articles by foreign-trained students and famous writers, leaving parochial people like Mao to discuss only such trivial subjects as the cigarette tax, the Hunan provincial constitution, the role of the merchants in the Peking Coup of 1923, and so on. For lack of experience of living and working in great industrial cities like Shanghai and Canton, he was in no position to match the abilities of the seasoned labor leaders like Li Li-san, Chang Kuo-t'ao, and Liu Shao-ch'i. Indeed, throughout his whole political career, Mao has written only one solitary article on the labor movement—"Introducing the *Chinese Worker*"; and it runs one and a half pages long in his *Selected Works!* His total failure in urban work can be seen in his complete exclusion from the nation-wide urban movement against British and Japanese imperialism in May and June, 1925.

In withdrawing from active politics into his convalescence, Mao observed at first hand the peasant movement in Hunan.[22] This, in conjunction with Lenin's works and the Comintern's resolutions and directives on the peasants, not forgetting P'eng Pai's rural agitation in Kwangtung, revealed to Mao a source of revolutionary force that was perhaps more robust, certainly more numerous, than that of the Chinese proletariat. He never looked back from this discovery. Early in 1927, his famous "Report on the Investigation of the Peasant Movement in Hunan" was published. To begin with, the Report makes it clear that the revolutionary parties, the KMT and CCP, had not yet decided whether to lead the peasants, to trail behind them gesticulating and criticizing, or to stand in their way and oppose them.[23] That there was no party leadership of any kind in the Hunan peasant movement was unambiguously stated in an anonymous article carried in No. 199 of the *Guide Weekly (Hsiang*

<hr/>

[21] For his feeling of uncertainty and strong reaction growing out of these, see below, "A Talk in Hangchow," p. 107.

[22] E. Snow, *Red Star Over China* (London, 1937), p. 157, and Mao Tse-tung, *Hsüan-chi* [hereafter *HC*], 1947 supplement, p. 37.

[23] The *Guide Weekly* [Hsiang-tao], No. 191, p. 2062, or Mao Tse-tung, *Selected Works* [hereafter *SW*] (Peking, 1961), I, 24.

*tao*, p. 2194) of the CCP—"the party has lagged behind!" Mao was to echo this sentiment in his speech on the question of rural co-operativization in 1955: "Members of the party have lagged behind the masses, like women with bound feet." [24]

If it was not the party, then who was leading the Hunan peasants? Mao spoke of the poor peasants' "doing all the organization and revolutionary work." [25] Because they were the most revolutionary, they had gained the leadership of the peasant associations.[26] These people were the so-called riffraff, who were even able in some cases to win over landlords' militia forces.[27] They also had a crude understanding of the Three Principles of the People invented by Sun Yat-sen and of anti-imperialism.[28] Such adventurism and political consciousness were uncommon among the fatalistic and obedient peasants. Possession of these qualities made these people, whoever they were, abler than the ordinary poor peasants. To win over the militia, for instance, required some connection with its leaders and instructors, who traditionally were members of secret societies. Thus in the case of Hunan, these leaders of the peasant movement were most probably members of the Elder Brothers society. The activist elements among the poor peasants, or the riffraff, also almost certainly were members of the Elder Brothers, who actually were performing the role that the CCP and KMT ought to have played in leading the tamer masses.

Later in the year, after the split of the KMT-CCP alliance, Mao was sent back to Hunan and Kiangsi to organize the Autumn Harvest Uprising in which he relied upon the riffraff, army deserters, and the miners of P'inghsiang and Liuyang (the scene of the 1906 uprising).[29] It would have been surprising if he had not depended upon the Elder Brothers for supplies of men, arms, and money similarly to the way Ho Lung did in the Hung Lake region at the same time. After his defeat, Mao ascended the Chingkang Mountains, where he was faced with an entirely new set of problems.

[24] Mao Tse-tung, *Hsuan-tu* [Selected readings, hereafter *SR*] (Peking, 1964), II, 397.

[25] The *Guide Weekly*, No. 191, p. 2065.

[26] The *Guide Weekly*, No. 191, p. 2065 and *SW*, I, 33.

[27] *HC*, 1947 supplement, p. 25.

[28] *HC*, 1947 supplement, p. 31.

[29] Report from Hunan," in *Chung-yang t'ung-hsun* [The central correspondence], No. 6 (September 30, 1927).

An outlaw now, he had to organize defenses and set up a government, being without the guidance of his party from November, 1927, to April, 1928.[30] He, as the secretary of the Front Committee, *was* the Party.

Essentially, the problem was one of survival without surrender, which, in the absence of the Party had to be solved between Mao and the remnants of his army, on the one hand, and the peasants of the Chingkang Mountains on the other. This was a classic example of the situation envisaged by Trotsky: "The leading role of isolated communist groups in the peasant war does not decide the question of power. Class decide[s] and not parties." [31] Trotsky was right to stress the power of the masses in such a situation, but he overlooked the power of the armed elements of the class—the peasant army.

From this period to January 15, 1931,[32] Mao served most of the time as secretary of the Front Committee. In that capacity, he often wrangled with the Party Center over the issue of autonomy. As the leader of a local party branch, always dealing with fluid and urgent situations, Mao needed greater self-determination than the Party Center was prepared to allow. From the point of view of the Center, which was ideologically and politically under the guidance of the Comintern, central control over the regions was essential lest the revolution fall apart and dwindle into a traditional type of peasant war with no hope of victory. However, from Mao's point of view, the survival of the movement—that is, the survival of the revolution—depended upon its ability to win the support of the peasant masses, and consequently what the masses wish must decide everything. Without their support, the movement would be unable to preserve itself against the KMT's military attack or to obtain supplies of men and arms. It all boiled down to a question as to whether the party cadres or the masses should have the power of decision—an issue known later as "elitism *vs.* the mass line."

At this stage, Mao's perspective was confined chiefly to his immediate problems, the problems of the small but growing enclave

[30] *HC*, 1947 supplement, pp. 55–56.

[31] L. Trotsky, *Problems of the Chinese Revolution*, reprint (New York, 1966), p. 158.

[32] Wang Chien-min, *Chung-kuo kung-ch'an-tang shih-kao* [A draft history of the CCP] (Taipei, 1965), II, 503.

under his control; larger issues such as the organization and discipline of the Party and a form of proletarian hegemony had not
yet become compellingly relevant. They were perhaps still beyond
his perception. It must be remembered that Mao was then poorly
equipped as to theory to cross swords with the Moscow-trained and
better-informed leaders at the Party Center.

As long as the Party Center remained in Shanghai—perhaps for
the sake of a semblance of proletarian hegemony or for easier contact with Moscow—Mao could preserve a considerable measure of
autonomy. The extreme instances of his defiance were his refusal to
attend the conference of Chinese soviet areas in Shanghai in spite
of the Party's repeated urgings[33] and his withdrawal from the second attack on Ch'angsha without the sanction of the Party, an act
that caused the collapse of the Li Li-san's leadership.[34]

Replacing Li Li-san were the "28 Bolsheviks," headed by Wang
Ming and Ch'in Pang-hsien,[35] who were determined to redress the
topsy-turvy situation by the creation of a series of branches of the
Politburo in the major soviets. Because of this, the Front Committees
were rendered redundant and were abolished.[36] Thus deprived of
his secretaryship of the Front Committee, Mao still retained his
control over the army and the soviet government in Kiangsi and
Fukien. He ceded his military power to Chou En-lai in August,
1932, and his domination of the soviet government to Chang Wen-
t'ien in January, 1934.[37] During this period of fierce power struggles, Mao, almost as if out of spite, refrained from mentioning the
Party's role in the major military, economic, and political campaigns when he spoke in public. Lenin's substitutism of the Party
for the masses was not Mao's principle at all; it was never to be so.
In his capacity as the chairman of the national soviet government,
he consistently stressed the contributions of the army, of the soviets,
and of the masses. This negative way of getting even with the Party
leadership eloquently expressed a helpless man's bitterness against

[33] *Chung-kuo kung-ch'an-tang shih-kao*, II, 281.

[34] Jerome Ch'en, *Mao and the Chinese Revolution* (London, New York, 1965),
pp. 158–59.

[35] See appendix.

[36] Wang Chien-min, *op. cit.*, II, 503, 506.

[37] Hsiao Tso-liang, *Power Relations within the Chinese Communist Movement,
1930–1934* (Seattle, 1961), pp. 220–21. Chang Wen-t'ien even threatened to expel Mao from the Party. See below, p. 95.

a formidable opposition. All his pent-up hatred was to come out later when soviet power once more was firmly established in Yenan. It is worth noticing that Mao did not begin again to praise the role of the Party in the revolution in any unreserved manner until 1936,[38] after he himself had won control over the Party and his relationship with it had considerably improved.

The line of the 28 Bolsheviks was defeated by the disasters of 1934. The loss of all the central China soviets except Ho Lung's in northwest Hunan and the loss of two-thirds of the First Front Army (in the battle of the Hsiang River, on the first leg of the Long March) were enough, by any measure, to discredit the leadership of the 28 Bolsheviks. Their decline signaled Mao's rise to power. But his rise should not be interpreted as attainment of supreme control of the party organization, for there is new evidence that throws doubt upon Peking's official claim that Mao assumed leadership of the Party at the Tsunyi Conference of the Politburo in January, 1935.[39] Even if Mao was elected on that occasion to the chairmanship of the Politburo, the traditionally powerful post of Secretary General was occupied by Chang Wen-t'ien, a leader among the 28 Bolsheviks. Chang ceased to play a prominent role in the Party after 1939, but probably clung to the post until Liu Shao-ch'i succeeded him in 1943. Liu handed it over to Teng Hsiao-p'ing in 1956. In spite of the determining voice of the chairman of the

[38] *HC*, 1947 supplement, pp. 123–25.

[39] On that occasion Mao could not possibly have been elected to the chairmanship of the Central Committee, as the post was not created until the Seventh Congress, in 1945; furthermore, the Politburo, itself elected by the Central Committee, simply did not have such Constitutional power. Chang Kuo-t'ao might have been biased when he told Wang Chien-min that Mao became only the chairman of the government (Wang, *op. cit.*, III, 727). If this meant the chairmanship of the national soviet government, Mao had been in that post since 1931—a fact thus rendering Chang's statement meaningless. A Japanese scholar told me that according to reliable information from a Japanese Communist source, Mao acquired only military power at the conference.

There are these points to consider: (1) it is not clear whether the eighteen participants in the conference represented the majority required to elect a new chairman of the Politburo legitimately; (2) Chang Kuo-t'ao's defiance of Mao at the Lianghok'ou and Maoerhkai conferences of the Politburo might imply that Mao did not have the authority to coerce Chang; (3) the party machine continued to show disagreement with Mao before and after the Rectification Campaign of 1942–44. On these grounds, the Japanese information may well be reliable.

Politburo in policy-making, the implementation of policy, and the organization, training, and appointment of cadres, remained under the jurisdiction of the Secretary Generalship, which successively had been held by foreign-trained men. The fact that Mao has never held the post of Secretary General [40] makes his role different from Stalin's. Stalin derived his power from an elite force, the cadres; Mao's power derived from his ideology, his personal charisma, and his mass support, especially the support of the army. One of the decisions taken at the Tsunyi Conference was to go north, to be within striking distance of the Japanese, who had then extended their influence into Inner Mongolia, thus making the Communist advocacy of a war against Japan more meaningful. But, as Mao told André Malraux in 1965, "in the north, we found the possibility of contact with Russia, the certainty of not being surrounded." [41] As Sinkiang was then under the pro-Russian Sheng Shih-ts'ai, who was unlikely to interrupt communications between the CCP and Moscow, this reason for going north also carried conviction.

As soon as Mao and the Red Army settled in Yenan, they were preoccupied by two new, enormously important developments— Chiang Kai-shek's kidnapping in December, 1936, by the Manchurian troops and the imminent Japanese invasion of North China, which eventually was let loose in July, 1937. The formation of a united anti-Japanese front with the KMT and the designing of a military strategy became Mao's main concerns in 1936–38. Not until October, 1938, when the sixth enlarged plenum of the sixth session of the Central Committee was held, did he turn his full attention to a comprehensive survey of the problems facing the CCP. "On the New Stage" was the first political report he ever made to a plenum of the Central Committee, and it not only showed uncertainty in his political analysis, but also contained a number of platitudes and mistakes. To begin with, Mao promised to convene the Seventh National Congress of the Party in 1939, which, as events turned out, did not meet until 1945. Also, his prediction that the KMT would have a bright future was given the lie by facts. And finally, his discussions of Party problems (now reproduced under the title

[40] I suspect that this may be due to the liaison duties of the secretariat with fraternal parties abroad which would be awkward for a man of Mao's background and standing to fulfill and which might be a constraint on him.

[41] André Malraux, *Antimemoires* (Paris, 1967; London, New York, 1968), p. 533.

"The Role of the Chinese Communist Party in the National War," in the *Selected Works*) had an incredible number of mistakes that had to be drastically revised before republication. A question may be posed here: Was the text of the report as published in 1938 the original draft before the Central Committee's discussion of it, or was it a revised version finished after the discussion? If it was a revised version, why was it deemed necessary by the editorial committee of the *Selected Works* to revise it again so substantially in 1950–51? If it was the original draft, were the alterations made in 1950–51 based upon the discussion of 1938? After all, Mao himself has said that the report was "criticized, challenged, and doubted." [42]

In the report, Mao expressed the view that the role of a party cadre should be that of a vanguard and a model worker in the national war; he should possess all the attributes of a good fighter and administrator, should place the interests of the masses first (while subjecting his own to them), and should teach and learn from the masses.[43] Inevitably, Mao spoke of the mistakes in the past. He referred to Chang Kuo-t'ao and his line of policy in the harshest terms, as by this time Chang had already defected to the KMT. He also sternly denounced Ch'en Tu-hsiu's "right" and Li Li-san's "left" deviations. But when he came to the "left" deviation, the dogmatism of the line of the 28 Bolsheviks in 1934, Mao's words did not bite: "It must be pointed out that the mistakes then were not those of the general line of the party but of the people who implemented the line. Those people committed serious errors in military strategy and in the way they conducted the war." [44] Mao mentioned no names in this connection and merely went on to discuss how these mistakes could be avoided in future. As part of the answer to this question, he emphasized the need to study the theories of Marx, Engels, Lenin, and Stalin, as "in this respect, we are still far behind our brother parties in foreign countries." [45] He ominously added, as if to foretell what was to come:

[42] See the article *"Tang-ch'ien chü-shih ti tsui-ta wei-chi"* [The gravest danger at present], particularly its preamble, in the 1947 edition of the *HC*. The article is now included in the *SW*, II, under the title "Oppose Capitulationist Activity," but without the preamble.
[43] "Lun hsin-chieh-tuan" [On the new stage], in the *Wen-hsien* [The documents] (Shanghai, 1938), E.41–42.
[44] *Wen-hsien*, E.47–48. This sentence is deleted in the 1951 edition of the *HC*.
[45] *Wen-hsien*, E.47.

But Marxism can be translated into reality only through a *national form*. . . . There is no abstract Marxism, only concrete Marxism— i.e. Marxism in a national form or its application to the concrete conditions and struggles of China. . . . Therefore there is the need to *sinocize* Marxism. . . . Therefore the foreign "eight-legged essays" [party formalism] must be given up, empty and abstract themes must stop, dogmatism must be put to rest.[46]

A year later, writing an introduction to the newly created party organ, the *Communist*, Mao described his ideals for the CCP—"a bolshevized CCP which is national in scale, has a broad mass character, and is fully consolidated ideologically, politically, and organizationally." [47] Mao defined bolshevization under the conditions of war as: (1) the correct handling of the relationship between the Party and the bourgeoisie (the united front) and between the Party and the peasants (the peasant war) and (2) the consolidation and expansion of the Party in the meantime.[48] The *Communist* was created to further this purpose, but its influence was extremely limited. Apart from Mao's introduction, no article published in the organ ever has been referred to by any Chinese Communist writer. It was left to Earl Browder to cite[49] an article by Ch'en Po-ta in the January, 1944, issue of the *Communist*. The failure of this periodical to further Mao's cause may not be attributed entirely to the poor theoretical standard it represented; its attempt to sinocize Marxism-Leninism by having a Chinese "pontiff"—an effort that provoked strong opposition within the Party—may also have been responsible. The sinocization in this sense alone would imply a weakening, if not the severance, of the ideological tie between Yenan and Moscow and the possible growth of a personality cult around the man who was to evolve a new brand of Marxism-Leninism. The existence of such an opposition can be proved by Liu Shao-ch'i's speech on the intra-party struggle in July, 1941, in which Liu referred to members of the Party who "rely on resources outside the party to

[46] *Wen-hsien*, E.50, with my italics.
[47] *SW*, II, 285.
[48] *HC*, 1947 supplement, pp. 43–44.
[49] Browder's article is translated and published in the *Liberation Daily*, April 25, 1945.

engage in the intra-party struggle and *terrorize* the party." [50] What were the extraneous resources powerful enough to terrorize the CCP? The authority of Moscow?

The Party lacked discipline—a fact underlined by the defection of Chang Kuo-t'ao and the defiance of Wang Ming in the united front work in Central China. In the military sphere, P'eng Teh-huai and Hsiang Ying, leaders of the two groups of the Communists' armed forces, may also have treated Mao with disdain. From Mao's point of view, the need for an effective command system in the Party as described in his "New Stage" report was urgent. With the arrival of the new stage in the national war, the stage of a long stalemate, both the KMT and the Japanese could spare more troops now to deal with the growing influence of the CCP. The KMT troops formed a ring around the border region in North Shensi, causing dire shortages of food and of other daily necessities. The Japanese, on the other hand, launched their campaign against the guerrilla areas in their rear. The united front between the KMT and the CCP ceased to exist except in name. By the end of 1940, when the Communist New Fourth Army was ambushed by KMT armies, a crisis was at hand; a split in the front was imminent. It was clear that in such an eventuality, the CCP would need a leader of national stature to rival Chiang Kai-shek. As long as the united front continued to function and Sino-Russian relations remained effectively good, Mao could grow only under the shadow of Chiang Kai-shek and of Stalin. Now as a split was coming, Chiang's shadow vanished. Six months after the New Fourth Army incident, the Russo-German war broke out, and a year after that, Sheng Shih-ts'ai of Sinkiang turned against Russia and the Communists. Stalin's shadow suddenly shortened. This was an opportune time for Mao to put the Party in the order he wanted and to grow under the full blaze of the sun. Thus began the cult of Mao.

When Edgar Snow visited Yenan in 1936, he found "no ritual of hero worship built around him [Mao]." [51] When Lo Fu (Chang Wen-t'ien) wrote to celebrate the seventeenth anniversary of the

---

[50] B. Compton, *Mao's China: Party Reform Documents, 1942–1944* (Seattle, 1952), p. 212. My italics.

[51] E. Snow, *op. cit.*, p. 83.

CCP on July 1, 1938,[52] he carefully avoided condemning anyone (for example, Li Li-san) or praising anyone else (for example, Mao). Even Ch'en Po-ta, later a champion of the Mao cult, when writing in the *Liberation Weekly*,[53] paid no tribute to Mao, although he attacked Ch'en Tu-hsiu and Li Li-san. Significantly, he attacked neither Wang Ming nor Ch'in Pang-hsien. Up to then, the *Weekly* had published only one portrait of Mao in woodcut, on May 24, 1937. The Party as yet showed not a trace of any personality cult except that of Stalin.

But things began to stir at places other than at the Center of the Party. The president of the anti-Japanese military and political university, General Lin Piao, making a report on July 9, 1938, praised "Comrade Mao's leadership genius." [54] At the second conference of the representatives of the Party of Shensi-Kansu-Ninghsia Border Region on November 15, 1939, Kao Kang remarked: "The development of the national war in the past two years had proved to be completely correct the prediction of the three stages of the war made by Comrade Mao and the party Center." [55] And Hsiao San's article on Mao's youth published in the *Liberation Daily* on December 14, 1941, spoke of Mao as "our brilliant great leader, our teacher, and our savior." This was on the eve of the Rectification Campaign of 1942–44.

In this Campaign, Mao's prestige soared. Young propagandists— Chang Ju-hsin, Ch'en Po-ta, P'eng Chen, T'ao Chu, Jao Shu-shih, and Teng Hsiao-p'ing—seized the opportunity to show their loyalty to the new leader; erstwhile leaders—K'ang Sheng, Ch'in Pang-hsien, and Wang Chia-hsiang (all Moscow-trained)—toed the line. Among the eminent members of the Party, most military commanders conducted the Campaign as the Party instructed, but did not make any contribution to its largely expressionist literature. Chou En-lai was in Chungking preoccupied by his united front work, thus taking no part in it. Wu Yü-chang and Lin Tsu-han, the "elder statesmen," busy with their government work, made no special contribution either. Throughout the whole Campaign, there were only

---

[52] The *Liberation Weekly* [Chieh-fang chou-k'an] Nos. 43–44, pp. 65–69.
[53] The *Liberation Weekly*, Nos. 43–44, pp. 72–78.
[54] The *Wen-hsien*, I, G.6.
[55] The *Liberation Weekly*, No. 95, p. 20.

two conspicuously silent figures—Wang Ming and Chang Wen-t'ien. Simultaneous with the Rectification was the production drive in the border region and in guerrilla areas to ameliorate the food shortage created by the siege by the KMT and Japanese troops. In the drive, great publicity was given to Stakhanov-type heroes,[56] poor peasants who had greatly increased their agricultural output and thereby raised their standards of living. Although their successes were attributed in general to party guidance, a new note appeared in the form of special salutation to Mao, singling him out as "the star of salvation" of the Chinese people. Therefore Theodore White wrote after his visit to Yenan in 1944:

> [Mao] was exalted above ordinary mortals.
> Mao Tse-tung's personality dominated Yenan. . . . [He] was set on the pinnacle of adoration.[57]

And Chao Ch'ao-kou, a Chinese journalist who visited Yenan in 1946, observed:

> At present Mao Tse-tung's authority in the border region is absolute. . . . At any place of convention with a crowd of more than three, there is a portrait of "Chairman Mao." . . . Mao's calligraphy is found in every school or workshop. During this year's Spring Festival, Yenan bookshops sold more pictures of "Chairman Mao" than those of all the other important leaders put together. Not just more, but two or three times more.
> For workers and peasants, "Chairman Mao's" words are absolute[ly correct] and fool-proof.[58]

But the Party itself did not join the chorus of adoration in such an unreserved manner. The Central Committee's resolution on investigation and research of August 1, 1941, did not mention Mao at all; nor did its resolution on the Yenan Cadre School on December 17, 1944, make any reference to Mao's thought.[59] News

[56] Mary Sheridan, "The Emulation of Heroes," in the *China Quarterly*, No. 33 (January–March, 1968), p. 50.
[57] T. H. White and A. Jacoby, *Thunder out of China* (London, 1949), p. 215.
[58] Chao Ch'ao-kou, *Yenan i-yüeh* [A month in Yenan] (Nanking, 1946), p. 64.
[59] B. Compton, *op. cit.*, pp. 69ff., 74ff.

about Mao did not automatically occupy the most prominent space on the front pages of the party organs as it does now; nor did Mao's articles always lead the other features in the party periodicals. The first move to study Mao's three essays—"On the Protracted War," "On the New Stage," and "On New Democracy"—was taken not in Yenan, but by the party branch in the Shansi-Suiyuan area. Moreover, Mao's *Selected Works* never were published in Yenan; all the early editions (1944–48) were issued in the Shansi-Chahar-Hopei area under Nieh Jung-chen or in Harbin under Lin Piao. Not until April, 1945, at the last plenum of the sixth session of the Central Committee and the Seventh Congress was Mao able to have the history of the Party written in the way he wanted and to have his thought incorporated in the Constitution of the Party as one of its guiding principles. These remarkable achievements, to be sure, meant the Party's acknowledgement of the correctness of his revolutionary strategy and political line. Ideological authority, nevertheless, did not mean unhampered exercise of power in the party hierarchy. The chairman of the Politburo, after all, could hardly treat the Secretary General as just one of his underlings, and there is no evidence to show that since 1935 the power of the Secretary General had been severely curtailed in any way by the Party's successive constitutions.

The Rectification of 1942–44, which culminated in the convocation of the Seventh Congress, was not a reorganization of the Party; it attempted to sinocize Marxism-Leninism, and this in turn led to the establishment of Mao's ideological supremacy. Ideological leadership, as J. W. Lewis points out,[60] is not a matter of power, but a matter of relationship between the leader and the led. When its ideology was sinocized, the Party's attitudes toward the masses and its styles of work also were sinocized. The Seventh Congress also marked the CCP's coming of age, achieving its complete independence by recognizing that China's Party now had its own guiding principle that was as authoritative as Marxism-Leninism. Although authority is not power, power cannot be exercised legitimately without the sanction of authority!

Another meaning of the sinocization was the reorientation of the Party's attitude toward the masses. The search for the masses by

[60] J. W. Lewis, *Leadership in Communist China* (Ithaca, N.Y., 1963), p. 75.

any revolutionary leadership is closely bound up with its strategy for the revolution. In the classical Franco-Russian model—i.e. urban uprisings for a rapid seizure of power, to be followed by a period of struggle against reaction—the leadership needs mass participation as long as the uprisings and war against reaction last. If the revolution develops into a protracted war (in China it lasted 22 years), the leadership has to devise ways and means not only to fan the flame of revolt but to sustain and consolidate it. The problems of the masses in the latter type of revolution are vastly different and harder to tackle. The way Mao tackled them is known as the mass line.

Once a revolutionary begins to think in terms of revolutionary masses and their oppressors, as Mao did in the closing years of the 1920's, he opens his mind to some kind of class analysis. This is inevitable. He must first have complete faith in the capability of the masses, as Mao said in 1945: "The people, and the people alone, are the motive force in the making of world history." [61] Then he must define which groups among the people are his main forces, which are his allies, and which are his foes. These definitions necessarily are flexible, depending largely upon the strategical aims in a given phase of the revolution for their acceptable interpretations.

The Marxist-Leninist class analysis, which Chinese revolutionaries accepted after World War I, gave as historically inevitable a proletarian hegemony in both the bourgeois and socialist revolution of the imperialist era. Although the Russian proletariat before 1917 was weak, Lenin's substitution of the Party for the class worked well enough to achieve the overthrow of the Tsardom. When applied to China, a country whose proletariat was even weaker than its counterpart in Tsarist Russia, the elitist Communist Party was by itself more or less impotent despite aid from the Soviet Union. This is not to say, however, that the party leadership had entirely ignored the masses prior to Mao's ascendancy. The political resolution of the Sixth Congress of the CCP held in Moscow, July, 1928, emphasized the need to win over the workers, peasants, and soldiers (the traditional Russian pattern of alliance), so as to stage armed uprisings (the traditional Russian pattern of

[61] *SW*, III, 257.

revolution). However, the hegemony was still ascribed to the almost non-existent proletariat, whose vanguard was the Party. This was the mass policy of Li Li-san. The political resolution of the fifth plenum of the sixth session of the Central Committee on January 18, 1934, said: "The victory of the revolution depends on the party, the bolshevized line and work, the unity of thought and action, discipline and the ability to lead the masses, and the repudiation of any line that deviates from the line of the International and the CCP." This was the line of the 28 Bolsheviks. Both policies were appropriate to the revolutionary strategy of proletarian hegemony, urban uprisings, and attempts to win victories in one or several provinces. The reality of peasant wars and scattered rural soviets in remote parts of China did not budge Li or the 28 Bolsheviks from their views on the role of the masses and on the classical pattern of revolution.

Right from the beginning of the Chingkang Mountains soviet, Mao adopted a different view of the masses and gradually developed a line of his own, as has been briefly explained above. His essays on class analysis and land policies in the eight years before the Long March were written to clarify what he meant by the "masses" and how to rally them round the army and the Party. In his preface to the pamphlet on the village soviet work of Ch'angkang in Hsing-kuo, Kiangsi (December 15, 1933), in his analysis of the political mobilization and economic reconstruction of the same soviet,[62] and in his concluding speech at the end of the second national congress of the soviets,[63] mass mobilization remained Mao's central theme throughout. In a rural context, the masses would have to be the poor and middle peasants whose initial support of the Red Army and of the Party could be consolidated only by material improvements, such as land redistribution and political indoctrination. This would be the firm mass base of the Chinese revolutionary movement, not the non-existent proletariat. Upon this base, the revolution would proceed to encircle the cities in a protracted war. Protraction would make the sustaining of revolutionary zeal crucial both as to principle and technique. If this zeal flagged, blame could not be laid upon the masses lest they be alienated,

[62] *Tou-cheng* [The struggle], No. 42.
[63] *Hung-se Chung-hua* [Red China], January 31, 1934.

causing certain defeat of the revolution; but rather, it should be laid upon the cadres whose job it was to keep the enthusiasm of the masses waxing. The cadres might run too far ahead of, or lag too far behind, the masses; in either case, the result would be their own detachment from the masses and the masses' detachment from the revolution. When this happened, the masses must invariably be considered blameless, whereas the cadres were too far to the left or to the right. Infallibility of the masses was, and still is, the basic hypothesis of Mao's mass line.

In order to win over the masses, "all correct leadership is necessary 'from the masses to the masses.' This means: take the ideas of the masses (scattered and unsystematic ideas), then go to the masses to propagate and explain these ideas until the masses embrace them as their own, hold fast to them and translate them into action, and test the correctness of these ideas in such action." [64] The spiral, as it were, went on till the optimum was reached.

This line of political work and organization was adopted as the official line of the Party at the Seventh Congress.[65] The man who moved its adoption was Liu Shao-ch'i.[66] But the mass line expounded by Liu, though largely conforming to Mao's ideas, subtly differed from them in two respects.[67] First, Liu stressed the inseparability of the organization line and the political line. "In spite of the possibility of a temporary disharmony between them, it is inconceivable that a correct political line is accompanied by a mistaken organization line and vice versa." [68] Second, he also stressed the inseparability of being responsible to the masses and of being responsible to the leadership—the Party—for the interests of the Party and those of the masses were one.[69] With these two differences, Liu was essentially an elitist, an organization man, and

[64] SW, III, 119.

[65] HC, III, 1125, or SW, III, 321.

[66] Liu Shao-ch'i, Kuan-yü hsiu-kai tang-chang ti pao-kao [A report on the revision of the constitution of the party] (Hong Kong, 1947), pp. 24–34.

[67] Compared with Mao's "On the Coalition Government," in which the mass line was once more stated in Chapter 5. But this chapter seems to have a style different from the rest of the essay. The character ho (and) appears with great frequency, whereas in the other chapters, it is hardly used at all. Generally speaking, Mao does not prefer this conjunction; he uses t'ung, yü, or chi instead.

[68] Liu, op. cit., p. 29.

[69] Liu, op. cit., pp. 30–31.

a Russian-trained cadre. Applying substitutism, Liu was actually sticking a primarily Stalinist party onto the Maoist masses. Was he unaware of the insoluble contradiction between Stalin's elitism and Mao's mass line, or was he consciously and honestly striking a balance between the two? This question may never be answerable. What is certain, however, is that as far back as can be traced, this is the origin of the ultimate split between Mao and Liu. The doubtful authorship of Chapter 5 of Mao's "Coalition Government" and Liu's additions to the meaning of the mass line once again underlined the fact Mao did not have as much control over the Party as has been previously assumed.[70] It was probably in this sense that Teng Hsiao-p'ing asserted in his report to the Eighth Congress of the CCP, September 16, 1956: "In our party, all important matters have been for a long time decided by a party collective not by any individual. This has been established as a tradition."

Few structural changes took place within the CCP between V-J Day and the proclamation of the People's Republic, a period during which all CCP leaders were preoccupied with the military struggle against the KMT and the foundation of the new state. Mao's personal stature increased steadily until he eventually replaced Chiang Kai-shek as leader of the nation. But at the same time, peace in Europe and Asia (except China) brought back Russian influence—and Stalin's—over the CCP. Postwar Russia was no longer "the socialist motherland," but the leading power of a bloc of socialist states, with the newly created Cominform and diplomacy in the conventional sense linking up their parties and governments respectively. Russia's old position as the ideological hegemon of a world-wide movement gave way to more substantial authority and power. The cold war and the detonation of her first atom bomb within a week of the founding of the People's Republic of China helped to enhance this authority and to accentuate its usefulness. China needed a powerful ally, and according to her ideological commitments as well as to the dictates of geographic location and economic circumstances, this had to be Russia and the socialist states—hence her policy of "leaning-to-one-side" and Mao's first trip abroad to Moscow in December, 1949.

The stories of Mao's arduous bargaining with Stalin and of his

[70] See below, "A Talk at the General Report Conference," pp. 94–95.

passive role in the Korean War are now well known.[71] When peace returned to Korea and the constitution of the People's Republic was being drafted, the intraparty struggle against Kao Kang and Jao Shu-shih—Party leaders in Manchuria and East China, respectively—was already under way. The first two of these events, coupled with the death of Stalin and the Chinese government's wish to consolidate its central control over the regions, may have caused the attack on Kao and Jao, in the first serious dissension among the top leaders of the Party since 1949. These events also may have prompted Mao to present to the Politburo on December 24, 1953, a resolution on "Strengthening the Unity of the Party." This was the first of several of Mao's major statements since his assumption of power in October, 1949, that never have been made known to the general public.

Following this statement, Mao did an astonishing thing; he suddenly went off on a holiday in March, 1954, at the very time when the fourth plenum of the Central Committee sat to discuss the Kao-Jao affair. The plenum was called to decide the fate of two of the most important leaders of the Party, and yet the chairman was absent because he needed a holiday! A year later, March 21–31, 1955, an emergency congress of the Party was convened to seal the destiny of Kao and Jao, and at it Mao made an opening speech, a part of which said:

> In dealing with all comrades who have made mistakes but are conscious of them and willing to improve themselves, [we] must not only watch but also help them. That is to say, we should not just watch how they rectify their mistakes by their own effort, but should help them to correct these mistakes. Man needs help. "Although lotus flowers are beautiful, they need the adornment of green leaves." "A fence must have three posts; a good man [hao-han] must have three secret societies [pang]." One needs assistance from others especially when one is in the wrong. To watch and wait for the guilty comrades to correct their mistakes is necessary; it is also necessary to help, help them to correct their mistakes. This is the only constructive attitude toward comrades. . . . We must understand the two aspects, collective leadership and individual responsibility, being complementary rather than contradictory. However, individual re-

71 S. R. Schram, *Mao Tse-tung* (London, 1967), pp. 262, 265.

sponsibility is entirely different from individual dictatorship which is against collective leadership.[72]

If this excerpt represents the spirit of the whole speech, the chairman equivocated on the Kao-Jao issue.

Simultaneous with that issue was China's rural transformation from primitive to advanced co-operatives. The gradualism adopted by the Party and the government up to 1955 was to a large extent the result of vacillation between radicalism and conservatism; but the possibility of an earlier and accelerated rural socialization movement was a likely topic for deliberation at the emergency Congress, and Mao scored a victory over such cautious leaders as the Minister of Agriculture, Liao Lu-yen.[73] Four months later Mao was in a position to make the crucial announcement, "On the Question of Agricultural Co-operativization." This change in China's agricultural policy led to the "Socialist High Tide" in rural China in 1955 and 1956, followed by the Great Leap Forward of 1958.

Between the High Tide and the Leap, the Party convoked its Eighth Congress in September, 1956, at which Mao played a surprisingly small part compared with his role at the Seventh Congress, in 1945. The political report, usually the most important report of a Congress, was made by Liu Shao-ch'i; the report on the revision of the Party's Constitution, as referred to before, was made by Teng Hsiao-p'ing; and the report on the Five-Year Plan was made by Chou En-lai.[74] The adoption of Liu's and Teng's reports was a sure sign of their authors' ascendancy in the Party, and as a result, the Socialist High Tide may have been temporarily checked. Perhaps partly because of this, a second session of the Congress was deemed necessary. This was convened in May, 1958, to hear the announcement of Mao's policy of the Leap.

The Leap must be viewed against the background of Khrush-

---

[72] The full text of this speech never has been published. This excerpt may be found in the *Mao Tse-tung ssu-hsiang wan-sui* [Long live Mao Tse-tung's thought] (April, 1967), p. 10.

[73] Liao Lu-yen, "Report on the state of agricultural production in 1954 and measures to increase present production," *Rural Work Problems of 1955* (Peking, 1955), pp. 10–23.

[74] The *People's Daily*, September 16, 17, and 19, 1956. About Mao's two-line leadership policy and his retirement in 1958, see below, p. 96.

chev's denunciation of Stalin and the first growth of the schism between China and Russia. Five months before the first session of the Eighth Congress, Mao already had expressed his difference with Russia and Yugoslavia through the famous *People's Daily* editorial "On the Experience of Proletarian Dictatorship," and a sequel to it was published three months after the first session.[75] The ideas in these editorials were expanded later into a long report known as "On the Correct Handling of the Contradictions among the People" (February 27, 1957). The *People's Daily* editorials cannot possibly have been written by Mao alone, for neither the style nor the contents lends support to this view. They are, as clearly stated in the preambles, the results of two sessions of Politburo discussion. The report "On the Correct Handling of the Contradictions" is, however, vastly different from the editorials with respect not only to their scope, but also to the scanty praise Mao gave to Russia and Sino-Russian co-operation. The choice of a venue for the report was, to say the least, odd. Mao read this report at a meeting of the Supreme State Conference, which, as a government organ, handled only administrative affairs. It is against both the Constitution and usage to make such an essentially doctrinal announcement as "On the Correct Handling of the Contradictions" through this channel rather than at an appropriate meeting of the Party, say, at a Politburo meeting.[76]

Mao's second visit to Moscow, after this report, served only to widen the cleavage between Russia and China. In response to the new situation, Mao sensed an urgent need for the country to accelerate its economic growth by relying upon its own efforts and resources. The conscious imitation of Russia in economic reconstruction and technological advancement was to yield to the more labor-intensive, less cost-sensitive, and more *Chinese* methods first developed during the Yenan period, the difference being that the scale was now far greater and mass mobilization was correspondingly far more extensive. This orgy of voluntarism and total dis-

[75] On April 5 and December 12, 1956, respectively.

[76] A comparison of Liu's political report at the first session of the Eighth Congress, September, 1956, with Mao's speech, "On the Correct Handling of the Contradictions," less than six months later, will reveal that they cover roughly the same ground, except for Liu's more elaborate discussion on economy and foreign affairs.

regard of cautiousness ended in failure and disunity, as witnessed by P'eng Teh-huai's severe censure of Mao's leadership at the now famous Lushan plenum of the Central Committee in July, 1959. Although P'eng was defeated, the strength of the middle group, headed probably by Liu Shao-ch'i and Teng Hsiao-p'ing, was enhanced.[77] As early as December, 1958, it was clear that the Leap had run into rough waters, and Mao announced voluntarily,[78] or otherwise, at the sixth plenum of the Central Committee that he would not stand for re-election as the Chairman of the Republic. 1960 and 1961 were years of true reticence and retirement for this restless soul. Not until September, 1962, was he able to break his silence by putting forward a far-reaching plan for the improvement of socialist education at the tenth plenum of the Central Committee. At this time, Mao's prestige was so low that P'eng Teh-huai, in his plea for a revision of the Lushan plenum decision against him, which ran to some 80,000 words,[79] still "viciously attacked Mao." And T'ao Chu published an anthology of his own essays in which he spoke of "the sun having black spots on it." [80] "The reddest red sun," to be sure, is Mao. At that time, both the Party and the People's Liberation Army were dispirited,[81] and the socialist education movement, designed to provide an answer to this, failed to arouse much enthusiasm.[82] None the less, with Lin Piao's loyal support and firm leadership in the army, it was still possible for Mao to launch an attack on "revisionism" in 1963 and to draw attention to the problem of revolutionary successors in 1964. Even so, from the end of 1964 to July, 1966, he had to be away from the seat of power in Peking most of the time, to plan for a more effec-

[77] The *People's Daily* editorial, August 16, 1967.
[78] See below, p. 56.
[79] The *People's Daily* editorial, August 16, 1967, and D. A. Charles, "The dismissal of Marshal P'eng Teh-huai," the *China Quarterly*, No. 8 (October–December, 1961), pp. 63–67.
[80] Yao Wen-yuan, "P'ing T'ao Chu ti liang-pen shu" [A review of two books by T'ao Chu], in the *People's Daily*, September 8, 1967.
[81] J. C. Cheng, ed., *The Politics of the Chinese Red Army* (Stanford, Calif., 1966), especially Lo Jui-ch'ing's report on January 10, 1961.
[82] C. Neuhauser, "The Chinese Communist Party in the 1960's: Prelude to the Cultural Revolution," in the *China Quarterly*, No. 32 (October–December, 1967), pp. 17–18.

tive return to power while appearing to be in ill health,[83] almost on the verge of death, perhaps to delude his opponents into a false sense of security. His swim in the Yangtze on July 16, 1966, and the news about his physical condition following that dramatic event reversed the earlier impression and had a stunning effect upon Chinese politics. The *People's Daily* withheld all news of Mao's swim for nine days before giving it a front page spread on July 25, 1966—a fact that eloquently betrayed the amount of tension and political struggle that must have been going on behind the scenes in this high Party organ.

From the death of Stalin and the dismissals of Kao and Jao in 1953 to his triumphant return to Peking in July, 1966, Mao's vicissitudes in the Party tend to suggest (1) that there have existed two schools of thought regarding the road of China's socialist industrialization—the Russian model and the Yenan model—and (2) that Mao's grip on the ideological leadership has never fully relaxed, in spite of the removal of his thought as a guiding principle from the party constitution of 1956, and that it now proves to be his most effective political capital. Once established, an ideological authority clutches tenaciously on man's mind and may be difficult to dislodge. No one in China has consequently dared to challenge Mao's thought openly; the most one can allegedly do is to "wave the red flag to oppose the red flag."

To illustrate the Party's inclination to emulate Russia in socialist reconstruction, one need only refer to the *Material for Study for Cadres* (Kan-pu hsüeh-hsi tzu-liao) issued by the Party Center in 1950. This anthology of treaties, statutes, and theoretical writings on 12 subjects contains a large number of texts by the classical masters and by Russian writers; there are only 16 pages of writings by Mao as against 41 pages by Liu Shao-ch'i. After all, even Mao himself counseled in 1957:

> In order to make our country into an industrial power, we must learn consciously from the advanced socialism of the Soviet Union.

[88] E. Snow, interview with Mao, the *Washington Post* and the *Sunday Times* (London), February 14, 1965. Mao gave the same impression of poor health to André Malraux in August, 1965. See *Antimemoires*, pp. 535, 548.

The Soviet Union has been building socialism for forty years, and we treasure its experience.[84]

However, if the country were just to emulate Russia, many of Mao's writings would become irrelevant to the political and economic practice of China. True, three volumes of Mao's *Selected Works* were published in 1951 to celebrate the thirtieth anniversary of the CCP; but the Mao-study drive that followed their publication to all intents and purposes petered out before the end of 1952. The next great wave of enthusiasm for Mao-study aroused by the publication of his "On the Correct Handling of the Contradictions" in 1957, for which he was hailed as "a great prophet," [85] gradually cooled off after Mao's resignation from the chairmanship of the Republic in 1958. This sporadicalness was due partly to Maoism's itself containing little that was relevant in a conventional sense to the industrialization and technological advancement of China and partly to its being designed originally to solve concrete problems many of which already belonged to the historical past. More significant, perhaps, was the fact that once in power, the Party controlled all channels of public communication. If these channels should be used to propagate Mao's thought throughout the length and breadth of the country in a continuous and rising campaign, the result would be the transformation of Mao's thought from an elitist ideology as defined by Franz Schurmann[86] to a mass ideology. Hypothetically, once in possession of Mao's thought, the masses would be able to test its efficacy by direct political participation, thereby elevating their level of political awareness and understanding to that of the cadres or even surpassing them. From the elitist point of view, this might entail the withering away of the Party with all the accompanying inconceivable and dreadful consequences. In the particular conditions of China, this would also mean the establishment of Mao's personal authority to an extent hitherto unknown and not permissible in the communist movement.

The victory of the revolution already had contributed to the

[84] "On the Correct Handling of the Contradictions among the People" (London, 1957), p. 15.

[85] The *People's Daily*, October 11, 1958.

[86] F. Schurmann, *Ideology and Organization of Communist China* (Berkeley, California, 1966), p. 18.

image of Mao's infallibility. The Party, with its record of setbacks and defeats, could make no such claim either before or after 1949. For Mao, the mistakes of the Party had been the results of an imperfect understanding of the wishes and conditions of the masses, a deviation from the mass line. Only the masses and Mao emerged unscathed—the masses because their wishes and conditions *were* the yardstick of correctness, therefore incapable of being wrong, and Mao because he was the champion of the masses. The identification of Mao with the masses therefore led to the curious equation of Mao's thought representing the people's will. To speak or act against Mao meant virtually to oppose the people and to commit treason.[87]

Specific though they were, Mao's writings did contain general remarks based on universal observations of both Chinese and European origins. They assumed, for instance, that the majority (usually put at 95 percent) of the masses were good in the sense of being "poor and blank," unspoiled by sophistication. They also assumed the malleability of man's nature through education and persuasion, including the use of criticism and self-criticism. Mencius and Wang Fu-chih, as pointed out above, were the forerunners of these views, which easily could be fitted into the framework of Marx's class analysis and dialectics, except that Marx and Engels might place greater emphasis upon the role of economic factors in shaping man's nature in contrast to Mao's reliance upon political indoctrination.

Under the given conditions of literacy and underdeveloped channels of social communication in China, the propagation of Maoism still depended to a considerable extent upon the service of "evangelists," who were formerly party cadres but since 1960 have been soldiers of the army. Promoted by the army under the command of Lin Piao, Maoism was presented as universal truth capsulated in a little red book, *Quotations from Chairman Mao Tse-tung*. The *Quotations* is comprised of epigrams, which are strongly reminiscent of those in Confucius's *Analects*. They were lifted out of their context in Mao's essays and rearranged for ready application to any and every problem that conceivably might face their users.

---

[87] Liu Shao-ch'i, Teng Hsiao-p'ing, P'eng Chen, and other fallen leaders of the CCP are all accused of the cardinal crime of being disloyal to Mao.

The army also promoted hero-types, which were invariably young (under 25), hence "blank" (politically pure or unsophisticated), and often not yet members of the Party. These heroes all were said to be inspired by Mao's thought, and their action was interpreted as the result of long periods of Maoist self-cultivation, rather than of simply "human" heroic impulses. The soldiers all were required to study Maoism in this way and to learn from the new hero-types. When this political training was completed, Mao had an organized force of four million at his disposal vis-à-vis the Party of over 17 million. The time was then at hand to call the nation to emulate the army. This campaign, in turn, set the stage for the Cultural Revolution.

What did Mao wish to achieve in the crisis of the Cultural Revolution, which was largely his creation? Article I of the resolution adopted by the eleventh plenum of the Central Committee on August 8, 1966 (alleged by the *Red Flag* and the *People's Daily* editorial on August 16, 1967, as being drafted by Mao), defines Mao's goals as follows:

> At present our aims are to topple the faction in power which has been following the capitalist road, to criticize the bourgeois, reactionary academic "authorities," to criticize the ideology of the bourgeoisie and all exploiting classes, to reform education, literature, and art, and to rectify all the superstructure which is incompatible with the socialist economic foundation, so as to consolidate and develop the socialist system.[88]

In short, his negative aims were to eliminate the opposition that was said to have been leading the country toward a "capitalist restoration" and to rectify both erroneous thought and structures, so that socialist reconstruction might proceed with fewer obstacles. The ideological vacuum created through these eliminations was to be filled by Mao's thought, and this was the positive aim of the Cultural Revolution. This resolution was heralded by the *People's Daily* editorial on June 1, 1966, in these words:

> The proletarian cultural revolution is aimed not only at demolishing all the old ideology and culture and all the old customs and

[88] The *People's Daily*, August 9, 1966.

habits, which, fostered by the exploiting classes, have poisoned the minds of the people for thousands of years, but also at creating and fostering among the masses an entirely new ideology and culture and entirely new customs and habits.

What were the "bourgeois," reactionary, and "revisionist" ideology and culture the faction in power was alleged to have been trying to preserve? Judging by Mao's negative criticism and positive proposals, they may be summarized in this way:

a. It has been said repeatedly that politics must take command over economic and other matters. To quote from Mao, "politics is the life-line of all economic work." [89] This is true only when one assumes that productive force is constantly developing and constantly struggling to break through the cage of productive relations. The modification or removal of the old productive relations must be done by political methods. Productive force, too, can be increased by political means such as greater output through greater productive enthusiasm by the application of the mass line in the light of the experience of Yenan. A recent example of this was whether China's agricultural collectivization should precede agricultural mechanization, or follow it.

b. There is also the question of whether economic incentives and the price mechanism should be allowed to determine man's economic activities and the allocation of economic resources. If these are given free rein, one commits, in Mao's eyes, the crime of "economism" and is on the way back to "capitalism."

c. If one does not allow economic incentives and the price mechanism to work freely, the corollary is to replace selfishness by public spirit. Rather than working for one's own benefit, one must work for the benefit of all.

d. Mao's well-known dislike of bureaucratism is founded upon the belief that it hinders the growth of productive force and becomes a vested interest in itself. It also widens the gap between physical and mental labor.

Economics taking command, economic incentives, free working of the price mechanism, and bureaucratic practice are what Mao meant by "revisionism" as far as governing a socialist state was

[89] *Chung-kuo nung-ts'un she-hui-chu-i kao-ch'ao* (Peking, 1956), I, 123.

concerned. Mao identified this with the Russian way of socialist reconstruction. A departure from it, therefore, meant a departure from the Russian way. In dismissing this experience as "revisionist," therefore irrelevant to socialism, Mao's action had a twofold historical significance. In the first place, it meant that having experimented with Western and Russian methods without marked success, China was searching for her own way to power and wealth in the light of the Yenan experience. In the second place, by excluding reference to the Russian experience of building socialism, Mao put himself back to where Marx and Engels had been—that is, a position of ambiguity with regard to both the vision of a socialist state and the way to reach it.[90]

Indeed, even when he was extolling the Russian experience, in 1957, he cautioned his audience "to use our heads and learn those things which suit the conditions in our country." [91] "Conditions in our country" was a phrase hackneyed by all Chinese thinkers before Mao except those who were in favor of total Westernization. Like them, Mao used it as a shield against dogmatic and indiscriminate borrowing from abroad. What are the "conditions in our country"? Mao, as far is known, never had explained them systematically. The most prominent of China's special conditions probably was that of a populous agricultural country with a comparatively small amount of other factors of production per head. The average income was consequently low; so was the average ability to save. In such a country, capital for industrialization could not be formed in either the Western or the Russian way if the country decided to be self-reliant or was compelled to be so.[92] It had to find its own methods.

Although, theoretically, Mao had accepted neither the Malthusian concept of overpopulation nor the Ricardian law of diminishing returns of land, as a practical statesman, he must have known and admitted the extreme difficulty of forming capital in a country as poor and as densely populated as China. His anxiety to accelerate the pace of agricultural socialization was proof of this. In pinning his hope upon agrarian socialization's working the miracle,

---

[90] See below, "On the Ten Great Relationships," pp. 65–85.
[91] "On the Correct Handling of Contradictions" (London, 1957), p. 15.
[92] *Quotations from Chairman Mao Tse-tung* (Peking, 1966), sec. 21.

Mao focused not upon the diminishing returns of land, but rather upon the inexhaustible productive potential of the Chinese people. Once they were imbued with the right sort of spirit, they would work wonders. The foolish old man, according to a traditional legend adapted in Mao's essays, could move mountains! China must not use monetary stimulants to get her people to work harder; she must use spiritual and moral incentives. The monetary incentive was not only "revisionist," but also expensive, whereas the moral incentive was both socialist and cheap. In Mao's vision, to achieve strength, China must first achieve virtue. To put it differently, if the Chinese people can produce more and consume less, the result will be a larger surplus for the formation of capital.

This was the reason why Mao's thought on economic reconstruction was highly moralistic, consisting of almost nothing but a corpus of moral tenets—"serving the people," "building our country through diligence and frugality," "self-reliance and arduous struggle," and so on. To be sure, this was a reversion to the rule of virtue, but not to the virtues of Confucius. Mao's moral standards and his use of them differed considerably from the old master's. Confucian morals were familial, whereas Mao's were national. What was filial piety to Confucius was comradeship to Mao, with the crucial condition that such relations were secondary to loyalty to the state. Confucius used moral standards he had set up for social stability, whereas Mao used those he had worked out for social progress. Confucian morals were therefore inhibitive, whereas Mao's were meant to be incentives.

The strategy Mao designed for the Cultural Revolution was both complicated and fascinating, yet far beyond the ability of this brief introduction to give it a detailed discussion. Here are a few salient points.

In Communist parlance, any revolution, including a "cultural" one, must entail struggle between a pair of opposites or contradictories. What was the nature of the contradictions in a cultural revolution? Mao defined:

> What should our policy be towards non-Marxist ideas? As far as unmistakable counter-revolutionaries and wreckers of the socialist cause are concerned, the matter is easy; we simply deprive them of

their freedom of speech. But it is quite a different matter when we are faced with incorrect ideas among the people. Will it do to ban such ideas and give them no opportunity to express themselves? Certainly not. It is not only futile but very harmful to use crude and summary methods to deal with ideological questions among the people, with questions relating to the spiritual life of man. You may ban the expression of wrong ideas, but the ideas will still be there. On the other hand, correct ideas, if pampered in hot-houses without being exposed to the elements or immunized against disease, will not win out against wrong ones. That is why it is only by employing methods of discussion, criticism and reasoning that we can really foster correct ideas, overcome wrong ideas, and really settle issues.[93]

These were the rules that Mao set out for handling nonantagonistic ideological struggles. For the rules to work well, two conditions would have to be fulfilled. (1) Ideological disagreements could arise either from ambiguity and lack of understanding or from willful refusal to accept a view on reasoned grounds. Mao's assumption of clearly definable right and wrong admitted only disagreements arising from ambiguity and lack of understanding as being of a nonantagonistic nature, for through the process of explanation and discussion, ambiguity and lack of understanding should disappear. If it were disagreement out of willful refusal on reasoned grounds, the inevitable question would be, What is the "right" view to do about the "wrong" one? Will it allow the wrong to continue to exist, or will it suppress the wrong after explanation and discussion? In the first case, the nonantagonistic contradiction will cease or become dormant and in the second, it will deteriorate into an antagonistic one. (2) It must always be possible to distinguish plainly an antagonistic from a nonantagonistic contradiction. Furthermore, it must always be possible for the "right-minded" and the "wrong-minded" to make this distinction with equal facility and accuracy. In other words, both sides of the contradiction know all the rules of the game and play it accordingly, the stronger side refraining from coercion, the weaker from conspiracy. As long as the weaker side plays by the rules, the stronger side will never be tempted to alter them to suit itself. Without this assumption, the danger for the weaker side would be too great and the game would hardly be worth the candle; the weaker side would learn sooner or later to retire from it and never take it up again.

In the Cultural Revolution, a total disagreement was said to exist between the "revisionist" and the "proletarian" world outlooks. In a country with "proletarian" dictatorship, the means of exploitation already were transferred to common ownership. With private ownership went the economic and political structures derived from it, which were said to condition man's mode of thinking. How then could the "bourgeois" world outlook flourish in such a country and threaten to lead it back to capitalism? The answer must lie in the "bourgeois" heritage—old institutions, old customs, old habits, and old intellectuals—and the importation of "revisionist" ideas. The heritage and importation were viewed by the Maoists as retardatory to the progress of socialism, whereas their complete obliteration through a series of struggles would imply the approach to unhindered progress. It was on this hypothesis that the theory of uninterrupted revolution rested; the result of such a revolution would amount to a total reconstruction of Chinese, and ultimately world, culture.

Did the disagreement between these two world outlooks arise from ambiguity, from lack of understanding, or from willful refusal? Ambiguity did exist from the point of view of Mao's opponents. Like Marx, Mao had not worked out the details of his socialist vision or the way to reach it. Since Mao had outlined no precise plan, but only vague principles, his opponents could not lack understanding of it; rather, there was room for various interpretations on the grounds of ambiguity. Therefore, in the eyes of Mao's opponents, this was mainly a nonantagonistic struggle similar to previous rectification campaigns; there was no question of fighting against Maoism as such. From Mao's point of view, the picture was different. There was no ambiguity or lack of understanding in his opponents' line, for the "revisionist" view represented by the Russian model was as clear as daylight for him to see and study; but there was a willful refusal on Mao's part to accept it on reasoned grounds. The disagreement, as is now well known, had existed for some time, and the question was, what was Mao going to do about it? His decision was to fight "revisionism" by other means than persuasion. Therefore, from Mao's point of view, this was essentially an antagonistic struggle. These two schools of thought on the Cultural Revolution were clearly expressed in the so-called "February Outline" of P'eng Chen and the May 16th Circular of the Central Committee of the CCP.[94]

In the first place, since they adjudged it nonantagonistic, Mao's opponents simply allowed the contradiction to remain unresolved. In the second place, still thinking in terms of nonantagonistic struggles, they sent out work teams in the usual manner at the beginning of the Cultural Revolution. When these teams came face to face with a new kind of opposition, they panicked and resorted to ill-considered and ill-advised tactics to cope with the extraordinary situation. A work team in Sian, for instance, had no knowledge of who might be behind the rebellious students. In an effort to discover the identity of the people behind the students, they used psychological torture on them.[95] Such methods were unjustified; the need for them suggested a conspiracy, which would be unconstitutional and uncongenial to a nonantagonistic struggle. The work team sent to Lank'ao in Honan was similarly astonished to find a group of peasants deliberately opposing the Party.[96] This opposition, strong and daring enough to challenge the Party's rule in 1966 without the Party's knowing anything about its intention, had to be the army. Later events bore out this suspicion. No other political force in China was so well organized and disciplined as to be able to carry out a nation-wide operation in such well-guarded secrecy. The party leaders, however, misjudged the rules of Mao's game and were outplayed right from the beginning.

In this struggle, Mao had completely reversed his strategic procedure. In the civil war, he encircled the cities from the countryside to defeat the KMT; now he had dealt a lightning blow to the urban political centers and captured several cities and provinces before spreading the revolution to the countryside. In his earlier

[94] See the alleged "February Outline," *Survey of China Mainland Press*, issued by the American Consulate, Hong Kong, No. 3952 (June 5, 1967) and the CCP Central Committee's Circular of May 16, 1966, in the BBC *Summary of World Broadcasts*, FE/2468/B/1–5. See also Mao's instruction on April 11, 1968.

[95] The *Far Eastern Economic Review* (Hong Kong), April 20, 1967.

[96] The *People's Daily*, February 2, 1968. Also Liu Shao-ch'i's alleged self-examination, in *Survey of China Mainland Press*, No. 4037 (October 9, 1967).

revolution, he relied upon the support of the poor peasants as his main force; in this revolution, he ultilized young students as the spearhead and the army as his main force. In his earlier revolution, his procedure was to set up a border region regime before winning the masses over to him; in this one, he adopted Lin Piao's procedure of winning over the masses before setting up his revolutionary committees.[97]

The task of leading such a revolution could not be given to cautious and experienced middle-aged people; it had to go to the "poor and blank," audacious, uninhibited, and ardent youth already organized in schools and in the army. The employment of the Red Guards might augur the beginning of the functioning of a new mechanism that would carry on the revolution uninterruptedly generation after generation, and generation against generation. So far this has been the only mechanism in view and it may transform the traditional class struggle into one between aging conservatism and youthful radicalism to a war of generations. It may still claim to be "proletarian" in character as long as the youth can justify their actions in terms of "proletarian" interests. It may be fought within or without the Party or even between the Party and the young masses, depending upon whether the Party represents an aging conservatism or a youthful radicalism, upon whether the conservative middle-aged party cadres are ready to abdicate in favor of the radical youth, and upon whether the rules of the non-antagonistic game remain unchanged.

What is likely to be the outcome of this, Mao's second revolution? At the time of writing, much is still uncertain, although the signs are that Mao and his supporters are winning. What can be said, with a measure of safety, at this stage concerns the establishment of Mao's ideological and personal authority. As has been mentioned before, the publication of the *Quotations* and the creation of hero-types are important innovations for the intensification of the Mao cult. According to the New China News Agency on

[97] *HC*, 1947 supplement, p. 89. This letter to Lin Piao, dated January 5, 1930, is reproduced in the *SW* under the title "A Single Spark Can Start a Prairie Fire" with considerable revisions. As this was written as a letter to Lin, all the third person plurals in the present version should be read as second person singulars.

December 25, 1967, by the end of that year, 350,000,000 copies of the *Quotations,* 86,400,000 sets of the *Selected Works,* 47,500,000 copies of the *Selected Readings,* and 57,000,000 copies of the poems by Mao had been issued. Before the Cultural Revolution, only 13 printing factories had been engaged in publishing Mao's works; in 1967, this number was increased to 181! In addition to this, Chinese propaganda media pour out millions of emotive, assertive, and evaluative words every day to enhance the attractiveness of Maoism and of Mao the man, comparing his thought to nuclear weapons, to sunlight, to timely rain, and its author to father, to savior, to the helmsman. The result is that in China, it is supposed that no one thinks beyond the common premises of Mao's sayings. The way the *People's Daily* and its contributors reason may be used to illustrate this point. On November 3, 1965, a date chosen at random, the paper mentioned Mao 14 times in six pages; on November 3, 1966, 107 times; on November 3, 1967, 310 times! Most of these references were to what Mao said rather than to what he did.

When applying Mao's thought, the user is on his own; so he alone is responsible for the mistakes (such as factionalism), although the glory of success always goes to Mao. Obviously no inconsistency or ambiguity on Mao's part can be admitted; there can be only lack of understanding on the part of the user. The lack of understanding may arise from two sources: first, the epigrams, having no context, may appear ambiguous; second, they are so general as to make nonsense of their classification in the *Quotations,* hence being clumsy to use and necessitating learning them by heart. Many of the items grouped under the heading "Youth" (Section 30 in the *Quotations*), for instance, can quite happily go into Sections 1, 10, or 29, on party work. The result is that the little red book is like a large bunch of keys—all similar and yet all different. The 700 million users of these keys may stand in the cold, impatiently arguing and fumbling in an attempt to find the right one for a particular keyhole. Factionalism may thus arise. Not unaware of this danger, Mao and his supporters have therefore established Mao-study groups, first in the army and then among the masses, trying to find the consensus, the use of the right key for a particular hole. The experiences exchanged at the study group meetings often are publicized through the mass media in the hope that a wider consensus may emerge.[98]

It is only a short step from absolute ideological dictatorship to absolute personal dictatorship, and this has been the trend since the summer of 1967.[99] Mao's ideological authority is based upon his claim to infallibility, and infallibility is the basis of his personal charisma. By building up his dictatorship in this way, he appears to have both the inevitability of history and the will of the people on his side to lend him perfect moral justification. Politically, Mao is now the rallying point of the loyalty of the nation, a position formerly held by the Chinese emperor. The need for this reversion to loyalty to a person rather than to an institution (the Party, for instance) may underline the Party's failure to bridge the gap between the masses and the government. If the Party really has become so bureaucratic that it has detached itself from the masses, it may have come to be divisive rather than a cohesive force in Chinese politics. By establishing himself as the leader of the people and his thought as the absolute authority in the people's minds, Mao has made himself the symbol of China's unity.

But the Party is not yet being allowed to wither away; its function as the "bridge," however, has been taken over by the revolutionary committees—an experiment that the CCP once tried in the northwest Hunan soviet in 1934.[100] These new committees, according to Article IX of the resolution of the eleventh plenum of the Central Committee,[101] are permanent organizations that supply the form for the three-way alliance between the revolutionary masses, cadres, and soldiers announced after the crisis of January and February, 1967.[102] By this device, a large proportion of party cadres are being saved, provided that they are prepared to rectify their thoughts, and large numbers of "advanced elements" of the masses are being funneled into the salvaged party organizations, thereby helping the Party reform itself. As commented the party organ of Shanghai, *Wen Hui Pao,* on January 20, 1968:

[98] I am indebted to Miss Sheridan for this idea.
[99] The *People's Daily,* August 24, 1967, and September 11, 1967.
[100] *Hunan chin-pai-nien ta-shih chi-shu,* p. 645.
[101] *The People's Daily,* August 8, 1966.
[102] The *People's Daily,* March 10, 1967.

Therefore we must not think that the work of reorganization of the party is solely the business of the party members. This is also the common and urgent demand by the broad masses of non-party people.

The significance of this editorial—and of the reports in the *People's Daily* on January 1 and 19, 1968, to the same effect—lies in their contradiction of both Stalin's definition of the Party and Mao's as the vanguard organization of the progressive elements of the proletariat. The role of the vanguard gives the Party the sole responsibility for solving the contradiction between the state and the masses in a socialist society. On the other hand, the current "initiative" of the masses in demanding the reorganization of the Party presupposes that the Party is politically backward and thus unsuitable for the role of vanguard and incapable of solving the contradiction between the state and the people. Even if the Party is preserved in the Cultural Revolution, its future functions are likely to be limited to routine administration and channels of communication between the masses and the central leadership. This might therefore lead toward the withering away of the Party in a socialist country.

Upon the bureaucratization of the Party, a gap appeared between the Party and the masses, and this gap is bridged, in the Cultural Revolution, by the army. As the most advanced political element in the Maoist sense, the army has taken over the role of the Party.[103] Will the army relinquish its political leadership and its control over the masses when the dust of the Cultural Revolution settles down? Previously, the Party was said to be able to control the gun because it had the masses on its side. Now that the masses are with the army, how can the Party continue to control it? Hitherto, the only force that has held the army in check is Mao's personal authority. When Mao goes, will Lin Piao be able to command the loyalty of all the armed forces?

A more serious consideration is the firmness of Mao's ideological authority after his death. Vague as it is, and in spite of the present

[103] The army is now hailed as the most important instrument of proletarian dictatorship. See also Mao's instruction to the Lin Piao army in 1967, ordering the army to support the broad left-wing masses. This instruction is printed in an untitled anthology of Mao's statements published in China in 1967, pp. 12 and 13.

effort to find a consensus for usage, it probably will be open to various interpretations when its author no longer is there to pontificate. Although Lin Piao's contribution to developing a technique for popularizing Maoism is considerable, his personal stature as a theorist is lower than, say, that of Ch'en Po-ta, not to mention Liu Shao-ch'i. It is highly doubtful that he will be able to wear the master's mantle so as to become the sole authoritative expositor of Maoism. If such a situation arises, will Lin be able to rally the loyalty of all the political forces in China? If not, will he rely upon the armed forces to enforce a measure of unity of the nation?

Worse still, because of years of leadership stability, or immobility, China is in dire need of younger talented people to succeed such giants as Mao himself, Chou En-lai, Li Fu-ch'un, K'ang Sheng, and so on. The promotion of such literary and artistic figures as Ch'en Po-ta, Yao Wen-yuan, and Chiang Ch'ing to positions of great responsibility and eminence suggests that loyalty to Mao overrides other considerations in selecting any man. It is also a sad commentary on the poverty of talents in China. At a juncture like this, when both state and Party are structurally weakened by the Cultural Revolution, the People's Republic has actually no firm institutional base. It is anchored on Mao's personal authority supported by the army and the masses. Mao's authority, in turn, rests on such brittle foundations as his claim to infallibility and his belief in the malleability of man. In the age of science and mass communications, a reputation for infallibility held today easily can be converted into notoriety tomorrow. If man is as perfectly malleable as Mao assumes, he can be shaped by Mao today just as easily as he can be reshaped by another ideologue, or skeptic, tomorrow. Mao's boldness may lead him to sainthood or may cause untold harm to his country. At seventy-five, he still is awaiting the verdict of history on the value of his work as a revolutionary and as a national leader. If he fails in his present attempt, what will become of China? If he succeeds, what will become of the world?

# Chronology of Mao's Political Activities Since March, 1919

Born in Shaoshanch'ung, Hsiangt'an, Hunan, on December 26, 1893 and married four times—to a girl four years older than he in 1907; to Yang K'ai-hui in 1921, who was killed in 1930; to Ho Tzu-chen in either 1928 or 1930; and to Chiang Ch'ing (alias Lan P'ing) in 1939. An-ying, his first son by Yang K'ai-hui, had been to Moscow twice to study before his death in the Korean War in 1951, and Yung-fu, his second son, also by Yang, may still be working in Hunan as a district commissioner. Ho Tzu-chen gave him five daughters, all of whom were left to the care of some peasant families in Kiangsi before the Long March. Chiang Ch'ing has given birth to two daughters—Mao-mao and Lina.

Mao had two younger brothers, Tse-t'an and Tse-min, and a younger sister, Tse-hung, all of whom were killed—Tse-t'an in March, 1935, Tse-min in September, 1943, and Tse-hung in July, 1930.

For details of Mao's personal life, see Howard L. Boorman, "Mao Tse-tung: the lacquered image," the *China Quarterly*, No. 16 (October–December 1963), Stuart R. Schram, *Mai Tse-tung* (London, 1967), and my *Mao and the Chinese Revolution* (London, 1965). For Mao's publications, see my bibliography of Mao's writings, in the *Kikan Toa*, Tokyo, August, 1968.

This chronology is devoted entirely to Mao's political activities.

**1919**

**March**     Mao gives a public lecture in Ch'angsha, capital of Hunan, introducing Marxism.

**June 3**    Mao and others organize the Hunan Students Union to direct strikes and the boycott of Japanese goods in response to the May Fourth Movement in Peking. The Union is disbanded by the warlord governor of Hunan, Chang Ching-yao, after the summer vacation.

**July 14**   Mao edits the *Hsiang River Review* and organizes the Problem Discussion Group.

**August**    Mao takes over the editorship of the *New Hunan*. The publication of both papers is banned by Chang Ching-yao.

| | |
|---|---|
| September | Mao begins his activities in the movement against Chang Ching-yao. |
| October | Mao is elected to the executive committee of the Association of the Groups of Ten for National Salvation. |
| November | Mao writes a series of articles for the *Ta-kung Pao* (a daily) of Ch'angsha on the suicide of a girl in her bridal sedan-chair. (It is either late in this year or early in the next that Mao reads the *Communist Manifesto*.) |

**1920**

| | |
|---|---|
| January | Mao goes to Peking to agitate for the removal of Chang Ching-yao. |
| July | On his return via Shanghai, Mao organizes the first Communist group in Shaoshan. Toward the end of this month, he sets up a bookstore, Culture Bookshop, in Ch'angsha. |
| August | Mao sponsors the Russian Affairs Study Group and the Work-study Scheme for students to study in Russia. |
| September | Mao and others found Marxist and Communist groups in Ch'angsha and also take part in the Hunan Self-government Movement. (Despite these activities and publications, Kung T'ing-chang does not feel justified in mentioning Mao in his article, "The new cultural movement in Hunan in recent years," published in the *Ta-kung Pao*, Ch'angsha, September, 1920.) |

**1921**

| | |
|---|---|
| July 1 | Mao attends the CCP First Congress in Shanghai. |
| August | Mao establishes the Self-Education College in Ch'angsha and organizes trade unions in Ch'angsha and Anyüan. |
| Oct. 10 | At the inauguration of the Hunan Branch of the CCP, Mao becomes its first secretary. |

**1922**

| | |
|---|---|
| May | Mao opens the Anyüan Workmen's Club, whose director is Li Li-san. Later in the year, he and Li set up schools for the Anyüan miners. |
| July | Mao misses the CCP Second Congress. |
| October | Mao leads the strikes of Ch'angsha carpenters and masons. |
| Nov. 1 | Mao is elected to the chairmanship of the Association of Hunan Trade Unions. The Self-Education College changes its name to the Hsiangchiang Middle School. |
| Dec. 11–13 | Mao discusses problems concerning the welfare of Hunan workers with the governor, Chao Heng-t'i, and other leaders of the provincial government. |

**1923**

| | |
|---|---|
| April | Chao Heng-t'i orders Mao's arrest; Mao leaves for Shanghai. |
| May | Mao works at the CCP Center in Shanghai. |

| June | Mao goes to Canton to attend the CCP Third Congress and is elected a member of the Central Committee. Ten days after the Congress, he goes back to Shanghai to work in the organization department of the KMT and that of the CCP (as he now holds two party cards). According to several sources, Mao at this time holds the post of the head of the organization department of the CCP, also specially in charge of the co-ordination of the policies of the KMT and CCP. |
| December | Mao sails for Canton to take part in the KMT First Congress. |

**1924**

| January | Mao is elected an alternate member of the Central Executive Committee of the KMT. |
| February | Mao returns to Shanghai to continue his work in the two parties. |
| November | Because of illness and his "rightist" tendencies, Mao is sent back to Hsiangt'an, where he is to stay for three months. |

**1925**

| January | Mao misses the CCP Fourth Congress, at which he is not re-elected to the Central Committee. |
| February | Mao moves to Ch'angsha where he is to stay for six months. |
| June | Mao takes a deep interest in the Hunan peasantry and begins to organize peasants' associations, presumably on his own initiative. |
| July | Mao leaves for Canton because Chao Heng-t'i, the governor of Hunan, threatens to arrest him. |
| August | Mao takes part in the KMT-sponsored training college of peasant movement organizers in Canton. |
| September | Mao joins the KMT propaganda department as its acting head and edits the *Political Weekly*. |
| December | Mao pays a short visit to Shanghai to agitate against Chao Heng-t'i's persecution of Hunan labor movement leaders. |

**1926**

| January | Mao attends the KMT Second Congress and is re-elected an alternate member of the Central Executive Committee of the Party. |
| March 20 | After Chiang Kai-shek's coup, Mao relinquishes his post at the propaganda department of the KMT and goes to Shanghai. |
| May | Mao is back in Canton to take charge of the sixth session of the KMT training college of peasant movement organizers. He remains in Canton till October.* |
| October | Mao sails for Shanghai where he probably takes charge of the newly created peasant department of the CCP. |

* (I am grateful to Professor David Roy for this information from the *Kuomin Daily* of Canton.)

| | |
|---|---|
| **Dec. 10** | Mao goes back to Ch'angsha. |
| **20** | Mao addresses the Hunan peasants' and workers' congress. |

**1927**

| | |
|---|---|
| **January** | Mao stays in Shaoshan for three days. |
| **Jan. 4–**<br>**Feb. 5** | Mao inspects the peasant movement in Hunan. |
| **March 10** | Mao takes part in the KMT third plenum of the Central Committee in Wuhan. |
| **April 27** | Mao attends the CCP Fifth Congress. |
| **May** | Mao becomes the chairman of All China Peasants' Union. |
| **August** | Mao leads the Autumn Harvest Uprising in Hunan as the secretary of the Front Committee of the CCP. |
| **September** | After the failure of the Autumn Harvest Uprising, Mao is detained by a militia group but escapes. |
| **October** | Mao establishes his revolutionary base in the Chingkang Mountains; meanwhile he becomes a wanted man (reward: 5,000 yüan). |
| **November** | Mao is dismissed from the Politburo and also loses his position as the secretary of the Front Committee. |

**1928**

| | |
|---|---|
| **January** | Mao defeats a regiment of Wu Shang's Eighth Division at Ningkang. |
| **March** | The Front Committee of the CCP is replaced by the Special Committee of the Chingkang Mountains Base Area of which Mao is the secretary. |
| **April** | Chu Teh joins Mao at the Chingkang Mountains Base. |
| **May 20** | Mao calls the Maop'ing Conference. |
| **July** | Mao is replaced by Yang K'ai-ming as the secretary of the Special Committee, but at the same time his place at the CCP Central Committee is restored by the Sixth Congress held at Moscow. |
| **August** | Mao leads a contingent to Chu Teh's rescue in Kweitung. |
| **September** | Mao and Chu return to the Chingkang Mountains Base, where Mao regains his position as the secretary of the Special Committee. |

**1929**

| | |
|---|---|
| **January** | Mao's troops invade southern Kiangsi. |
| **February** | Mao's troops invade western Fukien. |
| **March** | Mao and Chu take Tingchow, Fukien. |
| **April** | Mao disagrees with Li Li-san's strategy, and his troops take Kanchow. |
| **August** | Mao and Chu are active in western Fukien. |
| **November** | Mao's troops take Shanghang. |

| | |
|---|---|
| **December** | Mao calls the Kut'ien Conference of the Fourth Red Army. |

**1930**

| | |
|---|---|
| **March** | Mao's troops attack Kanchow. |
| **April** | Mao is urged to attend the conference of representatives of soviet areas, organized by Li Li-san in Shanghai, but he ignores Li's repeated summons. |
| **August 1** | Mao and Chu lead an attack on Nanch'ang which is repelled. |
| **September** | Mao pulls his troops away from the second attack on Ch'angsha, probably without the sanction of the Party Center. |
| **October** | Mao takes Chian and creates the Kiangsi Provincial Soviet Government. |
| **December** | Mao uses the forces under his command to suppress a mutiny in Fut'ien. |

**1931**

| | |
|---|---|
| **November** | At the party conference of the Central Soviet, the Provisional Center of the CCP led by Ch'in Pang-hsien and Wang Ming attacks Mao's "rich peasant line." |
| **December** | Mao begins his term of office as the chairman of the Soviet Republic of China, with Hsiang Ying and Chang Kuo-t'ao as his vice-chairmen. |

**1932**

| | |
|---|---|
| **August** | The Ningtu Conference marks the decline of Mao's influence in the Red Army. |

**1933**

| | |
|---|---|
| **February** | During the attack on the Lo Ming line, Mao's personal power in the Central Soviet is further reduced. |
| **June** | Mao launches a land investigation movement. |
| **August 21** | The project of a Soviet University is adopted, and Mao is appointed the first chancellor. But no more is known of this project. |

**1934**

| | |
|---|---|
| **February** | The Second National Soviet Congress held at Juichin elects Mao the chairman of the Soviet Republic of China. |
| **August** | With the deterioration of the military situation, the clash between Ch'in Pang-hsien and Mao sharpens. Mao may have lost his membership in the Politburo at this time.* |
| **October** | The Long March begins, and Mao regains his position on the military council. |
| **December** | Mao calls the Lip'ing Conference of the Politburo. |

* (This is Kung Ch'u's date; Chang Kuo-t'ao in his interview with Robert North gives an earlier one.)

**1935**

**January**  At the Tsunyi Conference of the Politiburo, Mao is said to be elected to the chairmanship of the Politburo.

**June**  The First Front Army under Mao and the Fourth Front Army under Chang Kuo-t'ao meet at Moukung; thus begins the struggle between these two leaders.

**October**  Mao arrives at Wuch'ichen in Shensi where his army makes a junction with Hsü Hai-tung's Fifteenth Army Corps. This brings his Long March to an end.

**1936**

**July**  Mao is interviewed by Edgar Snow with whom he discusses the political and military aspects of an anti-Japanese united front with the KMT.

**October**  Mao orders the Communist troops to stop fighting Chang Hsüeh-liang's Manchurian army.

**Dec. 28**  After the Sian mutiny, Chiang Kai-shek considerably changes his views of Japan. In response to this and following a letter from the CCP to the KMT, Mao publicly states the CCP's support of a united front policy against Japan.

**1937**

**January–April**  Mao conducts an investigation into Chang Kuo-t'ao's mistakes, resulting in the elimination of Chang as a potential challenger to his authority in the CCP.

**May**  In two statements at party conferences, Mao tries to consolidate the Party's support of his united front policy.

**July–Nov.**  In a series of statements, Mao outlines the CCP's political policy in the newly formed united front.

**1938**  (Throughout the year Mao concentrates on the strategy of the anti-Japanese war.)

**Nov. 5**  At the sixth plenum of the Central Committee, Mao severely criticizes Wang Ming's views on the united front. At this time or earlier, Lin Piao and Lo Jui-ch'ing, as president and vice-president of the Anti-Japanese Military and Political University, begin to eulogize on the "leadership genius" of Mao.

**1939**  (With the war moving toward a stalemate, the possibility of a peaceful settlement between China and Japan increases. Mao's main task is therefore to combat this tendency.)

**October**  Mao initiates a new party organ, *The Communist*, to deepen the understanding of Marxism-Leninism and of the practice of the Chinese revolution and to plan a new line of party reconstruction.

**Nov. 15**  At the second party congress of the Border Region, Kao Kang speaks of Mao's accurate prophecy in the past two and a half years.

51

**1940**

**January**   Mao outlines his vision of China in the essay, "On New Democracy," and continues to fight against a peaceful solution between China and Japan.

**August**   One demonstration against a peaceful solution is the Hundred Regiment Campaign of the Eighth Route Army.

**1941**

**January**   After a serious clash between the KMT and the Communist troops in south Anhwei, Mao appoints Ch'en Yi, Liu Shao-ch'i, and others to reorganize the New Fourth Army.

**March**   Mao launches the Rectification Campaign (*cheng feng*).

**August 1**   The resolution of the Central Committee on investigation and research makes no reference to Mao's writings.

**Dec. 14**   Hsiao San's article on Mao's boyhood and youth is published in the *Liberation Daily,* and Mao is described by the author as "the brilliant and great leader, tutor, and savior."

**1942**

**April**   Mao initiates a reorganization of the party organ, the *Liberation Daily.* Thereafter the ideological reform of the Party, known as the Rectification Campaign, is gradually brought to a high pitch.

**June 25**   The *Liberation Daily* carries an editorial entitled: "Salute Comrade Mao Tse-tung."

**1943**

**May**   Mao explains the CCP's decision to accept the disbandment of the Communist International.

**July 7**   Ch'en Yi pays tribute to Mao's "sagacious leadership."

**July 8**   Wang Chia-hsiang pays tribute to Mao.

**July 12**   Teng Hsiao-p'ing calls for the Party to unite around Mao.

**July 13**   Ch'in Pang-hsien calls for the defense of the CCP under the banner of Mao Tse-tung.

**July 17**   People of the north-west Shansi describe Mao as the savior of the Chinese people.

**December**   Mao, the hero of heroes, is hailed by the production heroes of the Border Region.

**1944**

**January**   Five thousand copies of Mao's "On the Protracted War," "On the New Stage," and "On New Democracy" are printed and distributed by the Shansi-Suiyuan branch office of the Politburo.

**Feb. 12**   Portraits of Chairman Mao and Supreme Commander Chu Teh appear together in the *Liberation Daily.*

**June**   Mao receives a group of Chinese and American newspaper reporters in Yenan.

| Sept. 23 | After the Japanese summer offensive, Mao lays down the CCP's policy in its negotiations with the KMT. |
|---|---|
| November | Mao meets the American Ambassador, P. Hurley, in Yenan. |
| Dec. 1 | The Central Committee's resolution on the Yenan Cadre School does not mention Mao's thought as a guiding principle in party training.<br>(The first edition of Mao's *Selected Works* is published in the Chin-Ch'a-Chi Border Region.) |

**1945**

| April 24 | Mao announces his views on a coalition government at the CCP Seventh Congress.<br>The revised party constitution adopts Mao's thought as one of the guiding ideologies. |
|---|---|
| August 26 | Ambassador Hurley flies to Yenan to invite Mao to Chungking. |
| August 28 | Mao flies to Chungking for peace talks with Chiang Kai-shek. |
| September | At a party given by the Sino-Russian Friendship Association to celebrate the new treaty between China and Russia, Mao meets T'an P'ing-shan and Feng Yü-hsiang after a parting of over 20 years. |
| Sept. 3 | Mao is the guest of honor at a banquet given by Chiang Kai-shek. |
| Sept. 6 | Mao and the Russian ambassador are invited to dinner by Chiang Kai-shek. |
| October 8 | Mao attends a farewell party in Chungking. |
| Oct. 10 | The Chiang-Mao agreement is published. |
| Oct. 11 | Mao flies back to Yenan to a tumultuous welcome. |

**1946**

| January–<br>Feb. | Mao publishes a series of articles on the discussions of the Political Consultative Conference, then in session. |
|---|---|
| June | Mao comments on American aid to Chiang Kai-shek. |
| July | While the KMT secret police are killing and beating up intellectual leaders, Mao sends telegrams to each of the victims or their families to express his sympathy. North China United College organizes a series of lectures on Mao Tse-tung. |
| August | Mao receives American journalists, G. Stein and Anna L. Strong. |
| Nov. 5 | The *Liberation Daily* reports on the propagation of Mao's thought. |
| Nov. 12 | The *Liberation Daily* carries an article on Mao's love of children. |
| Nov.–<br>Dec. | Mao comments on the civil war. |

**1947**

| | |
|---|---|
| **March** | Mao departs from Yenan as the KMT troops take the city. |
| **April** | Mao is at Wangchiawan. |
| **June** | The Nanking Supreme Court orders the arrest of Mao. |
| **July** | Mao leaves Yülin. |
| **October** | Mao announced the new land law at Chiahsien. |
| **December** | Mao makes the statement on the current situation and the tasks of the CCP at the Yangchiakou Conference of the Politburo. (Another edition of Mao's *Selected Works* and its supplement are published by the Chin-Ch'a-Chi Border Region.) |

**1948**

| | |
|---|---|
| **March** | Mao leaves north Shensi (thus bringing the famous Yenan period to a close) for Shansi. |
| **May** | Mao calls for a new political consultative conference. |
| **November** | Mao announces the numerical superiority of the PLA to the KMT troops. |
| **Dec. 22** | Mao demands that the KMT armed forces surrender. |

**1949**

| | |
|---|---|
| **January** | Mao refuses Chiang Kai-shek's peace terms and puts forward his own. |
| **April** | Mao announces the beginning of the period of "the city leading the countryside." |
| **June** | Mao addresses the preparatory meeting of the new Political Consultative Conference. |
| **June 30** | Mao outlines the fundamental principles of the new state in his speech, "On People's Democratic Dictatorship," and announces the policy of "leaning-to-one-side." |
| **September** | Mao opens the new Political Consultative Conference in Peking, which approves the Common Programme, while the KMT acting president, General Li Tsung-jen, orders the arrest of Mao. |
| **October 1** | Mao proclaims the founding of the People's Republic of China and is elected the Chairman of the Republic. |
| **December** | Mao leaves for Moscow. |

**1950**

| | |
|---|---|
| **January 2** | Mao arrives at Moscow. |
| **Feb. 14** | Mao concludes a Treaty of Friendship, Alliance, and Mutual Assistance with the Russian Government. |
| **Feb. 19** | Mao leaves Moscow. |
| **June** | A Mao-study campaign is launched, and Ch'en Po-ta writes "On Mao Tse-tung's Thought" to celebrate the thirtieth anniversary of the CCP. The campaign dies out in 1952. |
| **October** | Mao presides over the third meeting of the National |

Committee of the People's Political Consultative Conference.
(The work of editing and revising Mao's *Selected Works*
begins.)

**1952**

**October**    Mao inspects the Yellow River conservancy.
(The first three volumes of Mao's *Selected Works*
are published.)

**1953**

**February**    Mao does not take part in the fourth meeting of the
National Committee of the People's Political Consultative
Conference.

**March**    Mao commemorates the death of Stalin.

**December**    Against the background of an intra-party struggle against
Kao Kang and Jao Shu-shih, Mao proposes the strengthening
of the party unity at a Politburo meeting on the 24th.

**1954**

**March**    Mao is on holiday while the Central Committee holds its
fourth plenum to discuss the "anti-party" activities
of Kao Kang and Jao Shu-shih.

**Sept. 16**    Mao opens the first meeting of the National People's Congress.

**1955**

**March**    Mao takes part in a CCP Emergency Congress
which purges Kao Kang and Jao Shu-shih.

**July–
Dec.**    Mao launches the agricultural co-operativization movement
and the Socialist High Tide in the countryside.

**1956**

**April**    Mao participates in an enlarged meeting of the Politburo.

**May**    Mao swims across the Yangtze at Wuhan three times.

**September**    Mao presides over the Eighth Congress of the CCP
at which his thought is dropped from the party constitution
as a guiding principle of the Party.

**1957**

**September**    Mao inspects factories in Shanghai.

**November**    Mao visits Moscow on the occasion of the fortieth anniversary
of the October Revolution.
(Another Mao-study campaign is launched after the
publication of his "Correct Handling of the Contradictions
among the People," and this continues until his resignation
from the chairmanship of the Republic at the end of 1958.)

**1958**

**January**    Mao is in Chekiang.

**February**    Mao visits Ch'angch'un.

**March**    Mao tours Szechwan.

| | |
|---|---|
| **May** | Mao goes to the north and attends the second session of the CCP Eighth Congress in Peking at which the policy of the Great Leap Forward is adopted. |
| ✓ **June** | Mao is reported to have made the prediction that China will have her first atom bomb in ten years. |
| **July 31** | Mao welcomes Khrushchev in Peking. |
| **August** | Mao tours Honan, Shantung, and Tientsin. |
| **September** | Mao visits Wuhan and announces the creation of rural communes. |
| **October** | Mao goes to Anhwei. |
| **Dec. 1** | Mao takes part in a Politburo meeting in Wuch'ang. |
| **Dec. 12** | Mao declines to stand for re-election as the chairman of the Republic at the sixth plenum of the Central Committee. |
| *1959* | |
| **August** | At the eighth plenum of the Central Committee, Lushan, a fierce dispute develops between Mao and his critics led by P'eng Teh-huai and Chang Wen-t'ien with Mao's economic policy as the main target. This ends in the dismissal of P'eng. |
| **October** | Mao and Khrushchev celebrate China's National Day. |
| *1960* | |
| **May 3** | Mao receives Latin American, African, Iraqi, Iranian, and Cypriot friends in Chinan. |
| **May 7** | Mao is in Chengchow. |
| **May 14** | Mao entertains Japanese, Cuban, Brazilian, and Argentine guests in Wuhan. |
| **June 21** | Mao receives a delegation of Japanese writers. (The fourth volume of Mao's *Selected Works* is published.) |
| *1961* | |
| **April 28** | Mao receives Asian and African guests in Hangchow. |
| **October 7** | Mao sees Japanese visitors in Peking. |
| *1962* | |
| **September** | Mao presides over the tenth plenum of the Central Committee at which he calls for the consolidation of the communes and a socialist education movement. Neither seems to have aroused much enthusiasm. |
| *1963* | In a series of statements, beginning in August and continuing till May, 1965, Mao lashed at American "imperialism" while making veiled criticism of international "revisionism." |
| *1964* | |
| **Feb. 20** | Speaking to the French delegation, Mao blames Russia |

|              |                                                                                          |
| ------------ | ---------------------------------------------------------------------------------------- |
|              | for her "unilateral breach of the contract" between herself and China.                   |
| March        | The PLA under Lin Piao launches Mao-study campaigns.                                      |
| May          | *Quotations from Chairman Mao Tse-tung* is published.                                     |
| June         | Mao takes part in the CCP Work Conference and swims in the Ming Tomb Reservoir on the outskirts of Peking. |
| June–August  | Mao sees four new Peking operas.                                                          |
| August       | Mao specifies the five qualities of a revolutionary successor.                           |

**1965**

| January     | At an interview with Edgar Snow, Mao seems to be in poor health and remarks: "I am going to see God!" |
| April–May   | Mao visits the Chingkang Mountains.                                                        |
| July        | Mao receives General Li Tsung-jen and Li's wife.                                           |
| August      | Mao talks with André Malraux in Peking.                                                    |
| November    | Mao receives American friends and Japanese and Cambodian visitors.                        |
| Nov. 27     | Lin Piao issues five directives on the study of Mao's thought.                            |

**1966**

| July 16     | Mao swims in the Yangtze River at Wuhan.                                                   |
| July 21     | The *People's Daily* carries a report by the Afro-Asian writers who have watched the swimming competition at Wuhan, but there is no reference to Mao's swim. |
| July 25     | The *People's Daily* publishes the first report, with photographs, of Mao's swim.         |
| July 31     | Mao makes his appearance in Peking by attending a party given in honor of the scientists of the International Physics Colloquium. |
| August 1    | The resolution of the eleventh plenum of the Central Committee over which Mao personally presides is adopted and is known as the "Sixteen Articles." |
| August 10   | Mao and his "close comrade-in-arms," Lin Piao, seven times inspect the Red Guards and other forces of the Great Proletarian Cultural Revolution. |

**1967**

| | (Throughout the year Mao receives many visitors from abroad and has issued many directives on the conduct of the Cultural Revolution.) |
| April–June  | Mao sees three performances of the new Peking operas reformed by his wife, Chiang Ch'ing. |
| May 1       | Mao celebrates these three national occasions—the May Day, |
| July 1      | the anniversary of the foundation of the Party,           |
| October 1   | and the anniversary of the foundation of the People's     |

Republic—with the PLA, Red Guards, and the revolutionary masses. Liu Shao-ch'i, the Chairman of the Republic, and Teng Hsiao-p'ing, the secretary-general of the Party, are among the absentees; in the past they were present.

**September**  Mao inspects Honan, Hupei, Kiangsi, Chekiang, and Shanghai.

**Nov. 11**  The *People's Daily* publishes a new slogan: "Firmly establish the absolute authority of the great leader, Chairman Mao; firmly establish the absolute authority of the great Mao Tse-tung's thought!"

**Dec. 25**  Publication of Mao's works (number of copies):

| | |
|---|---:|
| *Quotations from Chairman Mao Tse-tung,* | |
| in different languages | 350,000,000 copies |
| *Selected Works* | 86,400,000 copies of complete sets |
| *Selected Readings* | 47,500,000 copies |
| *Poems* | 57,000,000 copies |

The printing of Mao's works has fully occupied 181 printing factories throughout the whole country.

## APPENDIX ON A TENTATIVE CHRONOLOGY OF THE POLITICAL BUREAU OF THE CCP

(According to Chang Kuo-t'ao, the *Ming Pao* Monthly, No. 22, p. 90, the organization was created in April–May 1927.)

**May 1927**  Chairman  Ch'en Tu-hsiu
Chang Kuo-t'ao, Chou En-lai, Ch'ü Ch'iu-pai, Li Li-san, Li Wei-han, Su Chao-cheng, T'an P'ing-shan, Ts'ai Ho-sen

**August 7 1927**  Chairman  Ch'ü Ch'iu-pai
Hsiang Chung-fa, Jen Pi-shih, Li Li-san, Mao Tse-tung, Su Chao-cheng, Teng Chung-hsia

**July 1928**  Chairman (?)  Hsiang Chung-fa
Chang Kuo-t'ao, Chou En-lai, Ch'ü Ch'iu-pai, Hsiang Ying, Li Li-san, Ts'ai Ho-sen

**January 7 1931**  Chairman (?)  Hsiang Chung-fa
Ch'en Shao-yü, Ch'en Yü, Chou En-lai, Hsiang Ying, Hsü Hsi-ken, Lu Fu-t'an

  alternates  Chang Kuo-t'ao, Ku Shun-chang, Kuan Hsiang-ying, Lo Tun-hsien, Wang K'e-ch'uan

**1932**  Chairman  Ch'en Shao-yü
Chang Wen-t'ien, Ch'in Pang-hsien, Chao Yung (K'ang Sheng), Liao Ch'eng-yün (Ch'en Yün), Wang Yün-ken

| | | |
|---|---|---|
| January 1934 | Chairman (?) | Ch'in Pang-hsien |
| | | Ch'en Shao-yü, Chou En-lai, Chu Teh, Hsiang Ying, Liang Po-t'ai, Liu Shao-ch'i, Mao Tse-tung,* Wang Chia-hsiang, Wu Liang-p'ing |
| January 1935 | Chairman | Mao Tse-tung |
| 1937 | Chairman | Mao Tse-tung |
| | | Ch'en Shao-yü, Ch'en Yün, Chou En-lai, Chu Teh, Jen Pi-shih, K'ang Sheng |
| April 1945 | Chairman | Mao Tse-tung |
| | | Chang Wen-t'ien, Ch'en Shao-yü, Ch'en Yün, Chou En-lai, Chu Teh, Jen Pi-shih, Kao Kang, Li Fu-ch'un, Li Wei-han, Lin Tsu-han, Liu Shao-ch'i, Lu Ting-i, Wu Yü-chang |
| October 1949 | Chairman | Mao Tse-tung |
| | | Chang Wen-t'ien, Ch'en Yün, Chou En-lai, Chu Teh, Jen Pi-shih, K'ang Sheng, Kao Kang, Lin Tsu-han, Liu Shao-ch'i, Tung Pi-wu |
| | changes | 1950 Jen Pi-shih died and P'eng Chen was elected to the Bureau; |
| | | 1953 P'eng Teh-huai was elected; |
| | | 1955 Kao Kang died in prison and Lin Piao and Teng Hsiao-p'ing were elected. |
| October 1956 | Chairman | Mao Tse-tung |
| | | Ch'en Yi, Ch'en Yün, Chou En-lai, Chu Teh, Ho Lung, Li Fu-ch'un, Li Hsien-nien, Lin Piao, Lin Tsu-han, Liu Po-ch'eng, Liu Shao-ch'i, Lo Jung-huan, P'eng Chen, P'eng Teh-huai, Teng Hsiao-p'ing, Tung Pi-wu |
| | alternates | Chang Wen-t'ien, Ch'en Po-ta, K'ang Sheng, Lu Ting-i, Po I-po, Ulanfu |
| | changes | May 1958 additions—K'o Ch'ing-shih, Li Ching-ch'uan, T'an Chen-lin; |
| | | Autumn 1959 suspensions—Chang Wen-t'ien, Ch'en Yün, P'eng Teh-huai; |
| | | Deaths—May 29, 1960 Lin Tsu-han, December 16, 1963 Lo Jung-huan, April 9, 1965 K'o Ch'ing-shih; |
| | | Spring 1966 suspensions—Lu Ting-i, P'eng Chen |
| August 11 1966 | Chairman | Mao Tse-tung |
| | | Ch'en Po-ta, Ch'en Yi, Ch'en Yün, Chou En-lai, Chu Teh, Ho Lung, Hsü Hsiang-ch'ien, K'ang Sheng, Li Ching-ch'uan, Li Fu-ch'un, Li Hsien-nien, Lin Piao, |

* Hu Hua, *Chung-kuo ke-ming-shih chiang-i* (Peking, 1959), p. 280, says that Mao was elected to the Bureau in January 1933.

Liu Po-ch'eng, Liu Shao-ch'i, Nieh Jung-chen, T'an
Chen-lin, T'ao Chu, Teng Hsiao-p'ing, Tung Pi-wu,
Yeh Chien-ying

alternates  Hsieh Fu-chih, Li Hsüeh-feng, Po I-po, Ulanfu

# PART ONE

# MAO LOOKS AT THE WORLD

*In selecting representative passages from the vast repertory of Mao's writings, one must bear in mind that he grew up in an atmosphere of intense nationalism (of both the introspective and the anti-imperialist kinds before and after 1919), that he was conditioned by the crude modern education he received, and that he led a successful and historically enormously important revolution. His Marxianization is admittedly of a higher degree than his Westernization, but even that has in no way adulterated his intense Chineseness.*

*The passages offered here are selected to show his sinocentric way of thinking, his fervor and astuteness as a revolutionary statesman, his vague views on culture and socialist construction, and his anti-imperialist and anti-"revisionist" vehemence. In the prime of his life, he was a master of modern Chinese prose and ancient Chinese poetry. These attainments also are represented here by the inclusion of his post-1956 statements as a contrast.*

*To compile an anthology of Mao's writings is by no means an easy task if one wants to avoid repeating what is already available in his* Selected Works, Selected Readings, *and* Quotations, *not to mention other collections of Mao's works published in the West. I have therefore chosen mainly statements of Mao's that hitherto have not been translated into English, original and unrevised statements that are textually different from those carried in the above-mentioned anthologies, and statements not readily obtainable by the general public.*

# 1

# China

## THE ROLE OF CHINA IN THE WORLD (1956)[1]

Things are always developing. In the forty-five years from the 1911 revolution—i.e. the *hsin-hai* revolution—to the present day, the appearance of China has completely changed. In another forty-five years, i.e. up to 2001 when we enter into the 21st century, the appearance of China will change again greatly. China will become a strong socialist industrial country. That is what China should be. She is a country of 9,600,000 square kilometers and of 600 million people. She ought to make a tremendous contribution to humanity. For a long time in the past her contribution had been meagre and this makes us feel ashamed.

But modesty is needed, not only now but also in forty-five years' time, and forever thereafter. In international contacts, the Chinese should firmly, thoroughly, neatly, and completely purge their great-nation chauvinism.

## THE CHINESE POPULATION (September 16, 1949)[2]

It is a very good thing that China has a big population. Even if China's population multiplies many times, she is fully capable of finding a solution; the solution is production. The absurd argument of Western bourgeois economists like Malthus that increases in food cannot keep pace with increases in population was not only thoroughly refuted in theory by Marxists long ago, but has also been completely exploded by the realities in the Soviet Union and the Liberated Areas of China after their revolutions. Basing itself

[1] From *"Chi-nien Sun Chung-shan hsien-sheng"* [In memoriam of Mr. Sun Yat-sen] November 13, 1956, in the *People's Daily*, November 13, 1966, p. 1. A fuller version of the same article may be found in the *Mao Tse-tung ssu-hsiang wan-sui* (April, 1967), p. 13.

[2] From "The Bankruptcy of the Idealist Conception of History," *HC*, IV, 1515–16, or *SW*, IV, 453–54.

on the truth that revolution plus production can solve the problem of feeding the population, the Central Committee of the Communist Party of China has issued orders to Party organizations and the People's Liberation Army throughout the country not to dismiss but to retain all former Kuomintang personnel, provided they can make themselves useful and are not confirmed reactionaries or notorious scoundrels. Where things are very difficult, food and housing will be shared. Those who have been dismissed and have no means of support will be reinstated and provided with a living. According to the same principle, we shall maintain all Kuomintang soldiers who have revolted and come over to us or been captured. All reactionaries, except the major culprits, will be given a chance to earn their living, provided they show repentance.

Of all things in the world, people are the most precious. Under the leadership of the Communist Party, as long as there are people, every kind of miracle can be performed. We are refuters of Acheson's counter-revolutionary theory. We believe that revolution can change everything, and that before long there will arise a new China with a big population and a great wealth of products, where life will be abundant and culture will flourish. All pessimistic views are utterly groundless.

### CHINESE AGRICULTURE

#### A Letter on the Development of Pig Farming
#### (October 11, 1958) [3]

Dear Comrade x x x:

This is a good document. Please consider it for publication by the New China News Agency. It seems that pig husbandry ought to be greatly expanded. Except among the national minorities who forbid the use of pork, the whole nation should imitate what has been done by the people's commune at Wang Ch'ien Ssu Temple, Wuch'iao, Hopei. In Wuch'iao, it has been easy to raise capital. Together with a correct policy and high enthusiasm, [pig farming] has been developed quickly. The crux lies in enthusiasm. Delays; all kinds of difficulties. This is impossible; that is too tough.

[3] From *Mao Tse-tung ssu-hsiang wan-sui* (April, 1967), pp. 21-22.

Such a world outlook belongs to cowards and idlers; it has nothing in common with the ambition of a Marxist-Leninist. Their style is roughly 180,000 *li* from that of a true communist. My advice to them is to think things over and correct their mistaken world outlook. I suggest that the party committees and branches of the provinces (and municipalities and autonomous regions), regions, counties, communes, administrative districts, production brigades, and production teams consider seriously the farming of pigs and of cattle, sheep, asses, mules, horses, poultry, and rabbits. They should plan and adopt concrete measures, and organize an animal and poultry farming committee (or team) consisting of three, five, or at most nine people. The leadership [of the committee] should go to a man who has enthusiasm, brains, and practical ability. In other words, he has to be a strong leader. The production of fodder is important. Among various kinds of fodder, it seems that sweet corn is the best. The Americans have done it this way; the Russians have begun to do it in a big way; Wuch'iao in Hopei of our country is following them. It makes us happy to see this. There must be many other places where pig husbandry is no worse than in Wuch'iao. The whole country must do it in a big and practical way and must give it the same priority as food grain. Sweet corn should be promoted to the status of a chief grain. Some people suggest that pig husbandry should be promoted to the top priority over all animal husbandry—no longer of the order "horses, cattle, sheep, chickens, dogs, and pigs." This I support by showing both of my hands. It is absolutely fair to give top priority to pigs. The great Russian expert on soil and agriculture, Wei-lien-shih,[4] emphasizes the interdependence of agriculture, forestry, and animal husbandry. All three should receive equal attention; none of them should be omitted. This is perfectly correct. We regard agriculture and forestry as the ancestors of the development of animal husbandry and animal husbandry is the child of agriculture and forestry. [In the process of development] animal husbandry [may] become the ancestor of agriculture and forestry especially agriculture, while the two become the children of animal husbandry. This is why the three are equally important and mutually dependent on each other. In the United States, grain cultivation and animal hus-

---

[4] This may be V. B. Veselovsky, the eminent Russian livestock specialist.

bandry are equally stressed; our country must follow this line of development, because it has been proved by experience to be successful. The main source of our fertilizers is pig and big animal farming. If we can achieve a pig a man or a pig a *mou* [1/6 of an acre], our fertilizer problem would be solved. It is chemical fertilizer [too], ten times better than any inorganic chemical fertilizer. A pig is a small chemical fertilizer plant. Furthermore, it has meat, bristle, hide, bones, and entrails (which have medicinal use). What stops us [from developing pig farming]? Fertilizers are the food of vegetables; vegetables are the food of animals; and animals are the food of human beings. From this point of view, pig farming and other animal farming on a big scale are decidedly justifiable. It seems possible to fulfill this glorious and great task in one or two five-year plans. Mechanization of agriculture is the (or a) determinant of the rapid development of the three-way alliance of agriculture, forestry, and animal husbandry. Since we have set up the Ministry of Agricultural Machinery this year, it seems that the mechanization of our agriculture can be attained in the not too distant future.

## SOCIALIST CHINA

### "On the Ten Great Relationships" (April 1956)[5]

To the Bureaux of the Center, the party committees of the provinces, municipalities, and autonomous regions, the party committees of all the central government departments, state and people's organizations, all the party branches and committees, and the General Political Department:

Comrade Mao Tse-tung's "On the Ten Great Relationships," written in April 1956, is a crucial document which admirably discusses the basic problems of socialist revolution and construction and gives important guidance to present and future work. Therefore it is printed and distributed to all members of the party above the county and regiment levels to study.

[5] From a collection of statements by Mao, no title, n.d. (probably 1967), pp. 19–28.

These are the notes taken when Comrade Mao Tse-tung delivered his talk. He has seen them and agrees to have them distributed for criticism, but he is not satisfied with them. Members of the party committees of all levels are hereby requested to make their views on them known to the Center of the party for reference when this essay is being revised.

*The Center*
*December 27, 1965*

In the past two months the Politburo has listened to reports on the work of 34 departments of the Center concerning finance and economics. After an exchange of views and several discussions of the Politburo, these reports have been summarized into ten problems, ten contradictions.

These ten problems were raised for one purpose only, i.e. to mobilize all the active factors and all the available strength for socialist construction in accordance to the principles of "more, faster, better, and more economical."

To mobilize all the active factors and all the available strength has always been our principle. Formerly, this principle was applied to winning the people's democratic revolution and terminating the imperialist, feudalist, and bureaucratic-capitalist domination. Now it is applied to a new revolution—the socialist revolution and the construction of a socialist country. It should be applied to the revolution as well as to the construction. This everyone knows. But there are some problems worth discussing. Some new factors and the defects and deficiencies of our work ought to be talked about and considered. By correctly handling these contradictions we may avoid taking unnecessary detours.

Let me read out the ten problems:

1. the relationship between industry and agriculture and between heavy and light industries;
2. the relationship between coastal and inland industries;
3. the relationship between economic and defense constructions;
4. the relationship between the state and productive units and individual producers;
5. the relationship between the Center and the regions;
6. the relationship between the Han and other nationalities;

7. the relationship between the party and others;
8. the relationship between revolution and counter-revolution;
9. the relationship between right and wrong;
10. the relationship between China and other countries.

All these are also contradictions. Contradictions are everywhere in the world. The world would not be what it is, if there were no contradictions.

Let me discuss these contradictions.

First, *the relationship between industry and agriculture and between heavy and light industries*

Heavy industries are the center of gravity and their development should be given the first priority. We all agree with this. In dealing with the relationship between heavy and light industries and between industry and agriculture, we have not committed any fundamental mistake. We have not repeated the mistakes of some socialist countries which attached excessive importance to heavy industries at the expense of light industries and agriculture. The results [of their mistakes] were an insufficient supply of goods for the market, a shortage of means of living, and an instability of the currency. We have given comparatively greater importance to light industries and agriculture. Unlike the market situation in some countries, immediately after a revolution, goods in our markets have been more plentiful. We cannot say that our daily necessities are abundant, but they are not in short supply. Furthermore, their prices, and the value of the *jen-min-pi* [the Chinese legal tender] are stable. This is not to say that no problems remain. There *are* problems—e.g. greater attention to light industries and agriculture than before, and adequate readjustment of the rates of investment in heavy and light industries and in industry and agriculture to give a comparatively greater weight to the investment in light industries and agriculture.

Does this mean that heavy industries are no longer important? They are still important. Is this to shift our focus of attention from them? Let me put it this way: most of our investment will continue to go to heavy industries.

What will be needed is more investment in light industries and agriculture. Let its proportion rise. Will this change shift the center of gravity? It will not be shifted; it will remain on heavy industries. The only difference is that both light industries and agriculture will receive a greater weight.

What will be the result of this? The result will be a more extensive and better development of heavy industries, of the production of means of production.

To develop heavy industries requires an accumulation of capital. Where does capital come from? Heavy industries can accumulate capital; so can light industries and agriculture. However, light industries and agriculture can accumulate more capital and faster.

Here a problem arises. Do you or do you not want to develop heavy industries? Do you want [them] badly or not very badly? If you do not want them, you would be doing damage to light industries and agriculture; if you want them but not very badly, you could invest less in light industries and agriculture; if you want them badly, then you ought to pay close attention to the development of light industries and agriculture. [Because] the more the output of daily necessities, the more the accumulation [of capital]. After a few years, there will be more capital available for heavy industries. Therefore this is a question of whether you sincerely want or just pretend to want [heavy industries].

Of course we all want heavy industries; it is quite out of place to say that we only pretend to want them. The only question is how badly we want them. If you really want heavy industries badly, you should invest more in light industries. Otherwise, you are not a hundred percent, only 90 percent sincere. In that case, you actually do not want them badly; you pay only some attention to them. If you take full notice of them, you ought to develop light industries carefully. Because, firstly, they can meet the needs of the people's livelihood and, secondly, they can accumulate more capital and faster.

As to agriculture, the experience of some socialist countries has proved that bad management could fail to raise production even after collectivization. Some other countries have failed to raise agricultural output because their agrarian policies were doubtful. They put too heavy a tax burden on the peasants and they lowered agricultural prices in terms of industrial prices. When we develop industries, especially heavy ones, we must give a proper place to

agriculture and adopt a correct agricultural tax and price policy.
Second, *the relationship between coastal and inland industries*
It is correct and essential to develop inland industries, but we
must also consider coastal areas.

On this problem, we have not made basic, grave mistakes. But
there are some shortcomings. In recent years we did not pay sufficient
attention to coastal industries. This, I am afraid, should be altered.

What [I] call "the coast" includes Liaoning, Hopei, Peking, east
Honan, Shantung, Anhwei, Kiangsu, Shanghai, Chekiang, Fukien,
Kwangtung, and Kwangsi. Seventy percent of all our industries,
also seventy percent of our heavy industries, were concentrated in
this area; only thirty percent were inland. If we do not consider this
fact, do not make a proper assessment of the industries in the
coastal areas, and do not fully utilize the productive potentials of
these industries, we would be making a serious mistake.

We must seize every opportunity to develop our coastal industries. I am not suggesting that all our new industrial plants should
be built along the coast. Ninety percent of them should be built
inland. But some can be set up along the coast. For instance, the
Steel Mill of Anshan, [the coal mines] of Fushun, the shipyard in
Dairen, the iron and steel and building material industries of
T'angshan, the chemical plants in T'angku, the iron and steel and
machine industries of Tientsin, and now the projected synthetic
petroleum industry, a heavy industry, of Maoming in Kwantung
(where shales of oil are found) are all situated along the coast.

From now on, most of our heavy industries, 90 percent or
more, should go inland so as to strike an equilibrium, a more rational distribution. This is beyond any doubt. Nevertheless, some
heavy industries in the coastal areas will have to be built or enlarged.

Our old industrial base is along the coast. If we do not take
enough notice of coastal industries, it will be to our detriment. Full
utilization of the equipment and technological potentials of the
coastal industries and careful development of them will enable us
to evolve and support the inland industries even more efficiently.
It is wrong to adopt a negative attitude toward coastal industries.
It not only hampers the full utilization of the coastal industries but
also hinders the rapid development of the inland ones.

We are in favor of developing our inland industries. The question is whether we are sincere or not. If you are sincere, not just pretending to be so, you must make fuller use of the coastal industries and build more [new] coastal industries, especially light ones.

From available information we can see that in some industries factories are constructed rapidly. Once they begin production and fully extend their productive potential, it is possible to recover the whole investment in a year. Thus, in five years, it will be possible to have three or four additional factories [of the same kind]. In some cases, two or three additional ones will be possible; in some other cases, one additional one perhaps. At least an additional half is always possible. In a similar way, this may also explain the significance of making use of our coastal industries.

Our long-term plan shows that we need 400,000 more technical cadres. These can be trained among the workers and technical cadres in the coastal industries. Technical cadres do not have to pass through the "orthodox" way (*k'o-pan ch'u-shen*). Gorky had had only two years in a primary school. Lu Hsün[6] did not graduate from any university. In the old society, he could be a mere lecturer, not a professor. Comrade Hsiao Ch'u-nü[7] had never been to any school at all. We must believe that skilled workers can become competent technical cadres through training in their practical work.

The coastal industries have a high technical standard, produce high quality goods at a low cost, and bring out many new kinds of products. Their development can lead to a higher technical standard and better quality goods of all the industries throughout the country. We must give full attention to this question.

In sum, without developing light industries, there cannot be an advancement in heavy industries and without utilizing coastal industries we cannot build up inland ones. Maintenance of coastal industries is not enough; they must be adequately developed.

[6] Lu Hsün (1881–1936) was a man of Shaohsing, Chekiang, the best known and the most sardonic of modern Chinese writers. Among his creations is the image of Ah Q in the *True Story of Ah Q*.

[7] Hsiao Ch'u-nü was a member of the CCP who taught at the Whampoa Military Academy and co-operated with Mao Tse-tung in training rural agitators in 1925 (Jerome Ch'en, *Mao and the Chinese Revolution*, p. 101). He was captured by the KMT and shot on April 22, 1927. See the *Ch'en-pao* (Peking, 1927) and *Hsien-tai shih-liao* [Source materials of contemporary history] (Shanghai, 1934), IV, second part, 319.

Third, *the relationship between defense and economic construction*

We must have national defense. Will it do to demobilize all our armed forces? No, it will not, because there are enemies who are "doing something" *(cheng)* to us, encircling us.

We have a considerable defense force. Since the anti-American war in aid of Korea, our military forces have grown stronger and our own defense industries have been under construction. Since P'an-ku separated heaven and earth [time immemorial],[8] we have never been able to make automobiles or airplanes. Now we have begun to manufacture them. Our automobile industries make trucks first, not limousines. That is why we have come to this meeting in foreign-made cars. We love our country, but our love cannot become effective quickly. It would be better though, if one day we could go to a meeting in cars made by ourselves.

We do not have atom bombs, not yet. But formerly we did not have airplanes or guns either. We defeated the Japanese aggressors and Chiang Kai-shek with millet plus rifles. We are already quite strong, but shall be even stronger. A reliable way [to achieve this] is to find out what is the adequate proportion of our expenses on defense. In stages we must reduce expenditure to approximately 30 percent of the total budget. [Meanwhile,] we must increase our expenses on economic construction, to accelerate and expand its development. On such a basis, our defense construction will progress faster. In this way, we shall have not only many airplanes and guns but also our own atom bombs in the not too distant future.

Do you want atom bombs? [If you do,] you ought to reduce defense expenses proportionately and spend more on economic construction. If you only pretend to want atom bombs, you will not reduce defense expenses proportionately and will spend less on economic construction. Which is better? This is a question of strategic aims which we must study.

At the third plenum of the seventh session in 1950, the question of cuts in government agencies and defense expenditure was raised and was regarded as one of three conditions for the improvement of our financial and economic situation. But in the first Five-Year

---

[8] Chinese mythology has it that P'an-ku lived in a "fused" universe for 18,000 years, before he separated heaven from earth.

Plan, defense expenditure took 32 percent, or one third, of the budget. This was too much. In the second Five-Year Plan, we must find ways and means to reduce this proportion so that we shall be able to allocate more capital for economic and cultural construction.

Fourth, *the relationship between the state, and productive units and individual producers*

Lately, we have discussed this question mostly with comrades from the provinces. As to the workers, their rate of production has been raised; so has the value they produce each working day. There should therefore be adjustments in their wages. It would be wrong if we did not notice this.

Since the Liberation, there has been a great improvement in the standard of living of the workers. This we all know. Some unemployed families have found jobs; some families which had one wage-earner now have two or three. I have met some families which were unemployed but now the husband, wife, and even a daughter have jobs. Their combined income enables them to enjoy a reasonable living. Generally speaking, our wage level is still low. But owing to more employment, low prices, and stability, the working man's life has changed beyond recognition from what it was before the Liberation. The working masses have maintained a very high morale.

What I have been saying is that we should pay attention to the development of the worker's initiative and morale. The problem of initiative and morale also exists in factories or productive units.

All things have their common and individual characters, or common and different characters. To have only common characters is impossible. For instance, our common character is to meet here. After the meeting our individual characters will prevail—some of us will take a walk, some read, and some others eat. Each one of us has his individual character. How can we go on with this meeting indefinitely? Do we want to kill ourselves with meetings? So, every productive unit or individual must have its initiative and individual character which are co-ordinated with the common character.

Is it better for the industrialization of the whole country if we give necessary benefits to individual producers and a certain amount of initiative to productive units? Of course, it is. If it is not, then we must not do it. It would be bad if we centralized everything, took away the factories' depreciation fund, or left the productive units with no initiative at all. On this question, we still lack experience. Many of our comrades here may also lack experience. We are studying it. There are so many factories and the number is growing. If we can fully mobilize their enthusiasm, it will be of great advantage to our industrialization.

As to the peasants, we have always maintained a good relationship with them. However, on the question of grain we have made a mistake. In 1954 [agricultural] output dropped because of floods, but we bought 70 million catties more grain. With the decrease [in the total output] [and increase] [in the amount purchased], the peasants became disgruntled. We must not think we are perfect. Lack of experience and understanding and the purchase of 70 million catties extra were our faults. Then we discovered our mistake. So in 1955 we bought 7,000 million catties less and arranged the "Three Stabilizations." [9] This was coupled with a bumper crop. An increase [on the one hand] and a decrease [on the other] gave the peasants 10,000 to 20,000 million catties more grain. The disgruntled ones calmed down and everyone said: "The communist party is really good." This is a lesson we must remember.

The peasants' collective economic organization is just like a factory—a productive unit. In such a collective economic organization, the relationship between the collective and its members must be adequately handled. Any inadequacy, a neglect of the peasants' welfare, will result in a failure of the collective economy. On this question, some socialist countries may have made their mistakes. In those countries, some collective economic units are fairly well run and others less so. When they are badly managed, agriculture cannot flourish. The collective must accumulate its capital. [On this] we must take notice not to demand too much from the peasants, not to make things too hard for them. Unless under severe conditions of natural disasters, we must as far as agricultural production allows see to it that the peasant's income is higher than that of the previous year.

We have discussed the questions of distributing summer and

[9] *"San-ting"*—the "three fixed": fixed production, fixed purchase, and fixed sales of agricultural products. See A. Donnithorne, *China's Economic System* (London, 1967), pp. 346ff.

autumn harvests with comrades from the provinces. The questions are: 1. How much to the state? 2. How much to the collective? 3. How much to the peasants? There is also the question of methods—the state by taxation, the collective by accumulation and management expenses, and the individual by sharing food and money.

All the assets of the collective are for the benefit of the peasants. Production costs do not need any explanation; management expenses are necessary; the sinking fund is for enlarged reproduction; the welfare fund is for the welfare of the peasants. We must discuss with the peasants how to find a proper ratio between the cost of production, management expenses, sinking fund, and welfare fund.

Both the state and collectives need accumulation [of capital], but neither should be excessive. Our method of accumulating state [capital] is through taxation, not through economic prices [manipulation of the price mechanism?]. In our country, the exchange between industrial and agricultural goods must follow the policy of minimizing the differentiation between [industrial and agricultural] labor, of exchange of equal values or approximately equal values. Our policies with regard to industrial goods are a low rate of profit, greater sales, and stable prices.

In short, we must consider the state and factories, the state and workers, factories and workers, the state and collective economic organizations, the state and peasants, and collectives and the peasants. We must not consider only one side [of all these relations]. There are some new points here and this is a big problem, as it concerns six million people. It must be given the attention of the whole party.

Fifth, *the relationship between the Center and the regions*

This is also a contradiction. In order to solve it, at present we must consider the development of local enthusiasm and let the regions do more work under the unified plan of the Center.

Judging by the present situation, I am afraid that it is necessary to expand the power of the regions. It is detrimental to socialist construction if regional power is too small. Our Constitution bestows no legislative power to the region; all legislation is done by the National People's Congress. However, in conformity with the policies of the Center, and within the law, the region can make rules and regulations according to the requirements of its work and local conditions. The Constitution does not forbid this.

The development of heavy and light industries needs both markets and raw materials. In order to fulfill this, it is necessary to consolidate the leadership of the Center, develop the enthusiasm of the region, and consider local interests.

Now there are dozens of hands interfering with local administration, making things difficult for the region. Although neither the Center nor the State Council knows anything about it, the Departments issue orders to the offices of the provincial and municipal governments. All of these orders are said to have initiated from the Center, thus putting great pressure on the regions. Forms and reports are like floods. This situation must change and we must find a way to deal with it.

There are two kinds of central departments which are concerned with regional affairs. The first kind can extend their leadership right down to enterprises. Their regional management agencies and enterprises are under local supervision. The second kind only lay down working principles and plans whose implementation depends entirely on the regions.

We must promote a consultative style of work with the regions. Nothing can be initiated by the Center of the party without having consulted the regions concerned. We hope the departments of the Center will take note of this. Everything must go through the process of consultation with the regions before an order is issued, if the matter concerns the regions.

We must have both uniformity and individuality. For the development of regional enthusiasm, each region must have its individuality congenial to its local conditions, which is at the same time conducive to the interests of the totality and to the strengthening of the unity of the country.

The provinces and municipalities have quite a few views concerning the departments of the Center which should be expressed. Likewise, regions, counties, districts (ch'ü), and villages have their views concerning the provinces and municipalities to which the provinces and municipalities should listen so as to arouse their enthusiasm.

The provinces, municipalities, regions, counties, districts, and villages should have their proper enthusiasm and proper individuality. The Center must not put them in a strait-jacket.

Naturally, we have to tell the comrades at lower levels that they must not act in an ill-considered manner; they must be considerate. What can be made uniform and should be uniform are to be made uniform; what cannot or should not will not forcibly be made uniform.

Two "enthusiasms" are better than one. We must fight for "the region," not from the point of view of regionalism or localistic interests, but from the point of view of the interests of the nation as a whole. We fight for what we should fight for.

The individuality permitted by the Center is proper individuality; it cannot be labelled "separatism."

To summarize, the region must have adequate power and this is helpful to building a strong socialist country. I am afraid that it is harmful to reduce the power of the region too much. We still lack experience in handling the relationship between the state and the regions. We are not yet mature in this respect. [I] hope we shall give this matter further discussion.

Sixth, *the relationship between the Han and other nationalities*

On this question, our policy has been stable, supported by the national minorities. Our emphasis lies on our opposition to pan-Hanism. Local chauvinism does exist, but that is not important. The important thing is to oppose pan-Hanism. The Han is our most numerous race. It would be extremely bad if we pursued a pan-Hanism against the interests of our national minorities. Therefore it is important to conduct proletarian nationalist education among the broad Han masses, to review the relationship between the Han and other nationalities. We had a review two or three years ago; now we must have another. Any abnormality must be re-adjusted and lip-service alone will not do. There are many people who speak about the eradication of pan-Hanism with gusto, but they do nothing.

What would be the appropriate economic management and financial systems in minority areas? This question needs to be studied.

The minority areas are vast and rich whereas the Han is a populous race. Underground in the minority areas there are buried many valuable deposits which are needed for our socialist construction. The Han must actively help the national minorities to carry on their socialist economic construction. By improving nationality relationships, we shall be able to mobilize all the factors, human as well as material factors, for socialist construction.

Seventh, *the relationship between the party and others*

This refers to the relationship between the CCP and the democratic parties and independent democrats. This is not a new problem. Since I have already referred to it, I might as well discuss it here. The question is: Is the one-party system better than a multi-party system? At present it seems that it is better to have several parties. This was so in the past and will be so in the future until the natural disappearance of all political parties. This long-term coexistence and mutual supervision of the communist and other parties are a good thing.

The first point is that all parties are products of history, to be found everywhere in the world. There is nothing which is not a product of history. The second point is that all historical products will eventually disappear into history. The communist party is a product of history and so one day it, too, will disappear, like the democratic parties.

Both proletarian parties and the proletarian dictatorship will vanish in the future. But they are absolutely necessary today lest we become unable to suppress counter-revolution, to resist imperialism, or to construct socialism. For fulfilling these goals, the proletarian dictatorship has to be coercive to a great extent. And this makes it necessary to fight against bureaucratism, against structural obesity. I propose a cut of two thirds of our party and governmental organizations.

Let us go back to the point under discussion here. The proposed cut in party and governmental organizations does not mean the elimination of democratic parties. We have a "forest" of democratic parties, quite a few of which have their own opinions about us. To these people, our policy is unity plus struggle, because we want to mobilize them to serve socialism.

[Political] opposition does not formally exist in China, because all the democratic parties accept the leadership of the CCP. In actual fact, some members of the democratic parties form the opposition.

On the questions of "Carrying the revolution through to the end," [10] externally leaning-to-one-side,[11] anti-America in aid of Korea, and land reform, these people equivocated. They had their own views on the question of suppressing counter-revolutionaries. They praised the Common Program and showed no interest in a constitution. But when the draft constitution was brought out, they raised their hands in approval. Things often go against oneself; this is certainly true of the attitude of some members of the democratic parties on a number of questions. They are the opposition and yet not the opposition. Their patriotism often turns them around from opposition to agreement.

The relationship between the communist party and the democratic parties must be improved. We must allow the democratic parties to express their own views. As long as they are reasonable, we would accept their views regardless of whose views they are. This would be a rational [attitude] for the party, the state, and people, and for socialism.

Therefore I hope our comrades will grasp the united front work. The secretaries of the provincial party committees should spare some time to review and reshape the situation and promote this work.

Eighth, *the relationship between revolution and counter-revolution*

What element is the counter-revolutionary element? It is a negative element; it is a destructive element; it is not a positive element; it is the opposite of a positive element.

Then, can a negative element be transformed into a positive element? Can a destructive element be changed into a beneficial element? Can a counter-revolutionary element be changed? This depends on social conditions. There are unavoidably die-hard, obstinate counter-revolutionaries. But under our social conditions the majority of even these people will change one day. Of course, some of them may not have enough time for their transformation

[10] *SW*, IV, 299–306. This refers to the period of peace negotiations from the end of 1948 to the beginning of 1949.

[11] *SW*, IV, 415–16. The CCP then decided to lean to the side of the socialist bloc.

before Yen Wang [Chinese Pluto] issues them an invitation. Others? Who knows when they will change.

Owing to the enormous strength of the people and our correct attitude and policy towards counter-revolutionaries—let them re-make themselves through manual labor—many counter-revolution-aries have stopped their activities. They take part in agricultural or industrial work and some of them even work usefully with en-thusiasm for the benefit of others.

A few points in our suppression of counter-revolution need con-firmation. For instance, the 1951–1952 suppression. Wasn't it neces-sary? There seems to have been a school of thought which regarded it unnecessary. This is wrong. We must admit that it was necessary.

Our methods of handling counter-revolutionaries are: execution, imprisonment, probation, and release. We all know what execution means. Imprisonment means to lock someone up and put him through labor reform. Probation means to allow someone to reform himself under the surveillance of the masses. Release means either to refrain from arresting someone if he is not a serious case or to free someone on the strength of his good conduct. To different cases different treatments should be applied; this is correct. These methods should be explained to the masses (*lao pai-hsing*).

Who were executed? What sort of people were they? They were the people the masses hated most; they were the people who owed a lot of blood debts. In a revolution of 600 million people, if [we] did not kill some ruffians, if we tolerated them, the masses would certainly disagree with us. To confirm that the killing of these peo-ple in the past was justified has its practical significance. It is wrong not to confirm it. This is the first point.

The second point to be confirmed is that the number of counter-revolutionaries has been greatly reduced. Although there is a law and order, [we] must not relax. It would be wrong to relax our vig-ilance and say that there is not a single counter-revolutionary left. There are still a few, doing their saboteurs' work. For instance, they have killed cattle, burned grain, destroyed factories, stolen infor-mation, and posted reactionary bills.

From now on, the suppression of counter-revolution must [follow the principle of] fewer arrests and fewer executions. Most counter-revolutionaries should be sent to agricultural co-operatives to do compulsory and reformatory labor. We cannot yet renounce execution; we cannot yet abolish capital punishment. If a counter-revolutionary kills someone or dynamites a factory, should we execute him? We certainly should.

The third point to be confirmed is to suppress counter-revolution in government agencies, schools, and army units. We must persist with the principle we adopted in Yenan: "Don't kill a lone wolf; don't arrest a crowd." Some are not executed, not because of a less serious crime, but because their execution would serve no useful purpose. It is better to let them live. What is the harm of not killing a lone wolf? If he can be reformed through labor, let him do that so that the useless can become useful. Besides, a head is not like a leek; it does not grow again once it is cut. If it is a mistake to cut off someone's head, there is simply no way to undo the mistake.

The principle of "Don't kill a lone wolf," [if] adopted by our counter-revolution suppression agencies, will not in any way adulterate the seriousness of our attitude toward counter-revolution. On the contrary, it will prevent us from making mistakes, irredeemable mistakes. This will free many people [from their worries]. The mouth must be fed, if the head is not chopped off. So it is necessary to find a living for the counter-revolutionaries, to show them a way to go. This will have a good effect on the people and improve our international image.

In the suppression of counter-revolution, there is still a long period of hard work waiting for us. We must not relax [our effort].

Ninth, *the relationship between right and wrong*

We must distinguish right from wrong both inside and outside the party. An important question here is how to treat the people who have made mistakes. The correct attitude is to allow people to join the revolution. "To punish [whatever mistakes have been committed] in the past so as to prevent them from recurring; to cure the disease so as to save the patient" is the attitude towards other people's mistakes we must adopt. We must help them correct their mistakes.

"The True Story of Ah Q" is a good story. I recommend those comrades who have read it to read it again and those who have not read it to read it. In the story, Lu Hsün describes in the main a backward, unenlightened peasant who is hyper-sensitive to criticism. He would have a brawl with anyone who criticizes him. He has a scabby head which he does not like to be reminded of. The more he dislikes it, the more people do remind him of it. The result is to get himself in a really tight situation. In the story Lu Hsün devotes a chapter to "Revolution Is Forbidden," describing how the fake foreign devil forbids Ah Q to revolt. In fact what Ah Q calls revolution is no more than looting. Nevertheless even this bit of revolution is impermissible.

Previously when the dogmatists led by Wang Ming dominated our party, we made this kind of mistakes. Anyone who did not suit their taste was charged with some kind of crime, and deprived of an opportunity to take part in the revolution. In this way they dealt severe blows to many people and did great damage to the party. We must remember this lesson.

It is bad to prohibit people from taking part in the revolution. It is also bad to prevent members of the party from correcting their mistakes.

We must allow people to participate in the revolution. Some say that we must watch how people rectify their mistakes. This is correct, but it is only half correct. The other half is to work on those people, to help them rectify their mistakes, to give them chances for correcting their mistakes.

In dealing with people who have made mistakes, we must first "watch" and then "help" them. We must give them work and help; we must not congratulate ourselves on the mistakes not being ours. Only factionalists would refuse to give work and assistance to those people.

Surely it is good for the revolution if there are more people in it. After all most of the people who have made mistakes can be corrected; only very few would persist with and repeat them. Having suffered from typhoid, one becomes immune to it. Likewise, having made a mistake, one learns from it, becomes cautious, and may not repeat it. We hope all those who have made mistakes have now got some immunity. It is those who have never made any mistakes who are in danger and have to be careful, because they do not have any immunity. It is only too easy for these people to stick their tail up.

We must be aware that excessive harshness applied to those who have made mistakes often rebounds on the applier. [It is like] picking up a rock and dropping it on one's own feet. One would fall and never be able to get up again. Sympathy with those who have made mistakes can help win their hearts. One criterion to tell whether a man has a good or bad heart is his hostility or helpfulness towards those who have made mistakes.

Right and wrong must be clearly distinguished. Once this is done, one can proceed to educate others and unite the whole party. Intraparty disputes, criticisms, and struggles are necessary. Under given circumstances, to apply an adequate dose of practical criticism, even a bit of struggle, is to help people correct the mistakes of oneself and of others.

Tenth, *the relationship between China and other countries*

We have put forward the slogan: To learn from other countries. I think it is correct. There is a type of leaders in our country who dare not or are unwilling to put forward this slogan. They need a bit of courage [which they can acquire] through getting rid of the kind of airs one normally sees on a stage.

Why are we willing to learn the strong points of all countries, all nations of the world? Every nation has its strong points. How else can it manage to survive and develop? To recognize that every nation has its strong points is not to say that it has no weaknesses. It has merits and demerits, strong and weak points. Our branch secretaries, and company or platoon commanders know from their notebooks that a meeting is called for nothing else but reviewing our experiences—i.e. our strong and weak points. These two points have run through a myriad years as well as this instant of time. The present period has its own strong and weak points; an individual has his strong and weak points. In sum, there are two, not one, points. To say that there is only one point is to know only one point, not both of them.

We propose to learn the strong points of other countries. Of course this does not mean that we learn their weak points [as well]. Previously, we had some people, rather muddle-headed, who learned even other people's weaknesses. Just when they had completed their learning and felt rather proud of themselves, the other people discarded those weaknesses. They fell on their face, like the Monkey King.

Some people do not analyze anything; they are guided only by "fashion" (*feng*). They adopt the northern fashion if it is fashionable today; they turn to the western fashion if it is fashionable tomorrow; and they return to the northern fashion if it becomes fashionable again the day after tomorrow. They have no independent views of their own. They are extremists, often swinging from one extreme to another. We do not want to do that; nor do we want to learn blindly. We must analyze and learn critically. We must not create a bias for copying any and everything foreign, for mechanically transplanting it.

For a time we had our dogmatism. We must wage a protracted struggle against it. In our academic and economic circles, traces of dogmatism still remain and these we ought to continue to criticize.

We raise the problem this way: The learning of the universal truth must be linked up with the reality of China. Our theory is the combination of the universal truth of Marxism-Leninism and the concrete reality of China. We must be able to think independently.

We openly put forward the slogan to learn from other countries, to learn all the progressive and good things from them, and to continue to learn from them. We openly acknowledge our weaknesses and the strong points of the others.

To learn from other countries entails the study of foreign languages, of more foreign languages.

I think our country has two weaknesses and two strong points.

First, we were a colonial or semi-colonial country under the oppression of imperialists. Our industries were undeveloped and our scientific and technological standard low. Apart from the immensity of our area, resources, and population and apart from the great length of our history, we were inferior to others in many things. We had nothing to show, nothing to be proud of. Long years of slavery gave us an excessive inferiority feeling. We grew unaccustomed to straightening our back-bone in the presence of foreigners. Like Chia Kuei in the opera, the Fa-men Temple, when he is asked to sit down he says that he is used to standing up, and does not want to sit down. We must do something about this. We must do something to raise the self-confidence of our people. We must do what Mencius said: "When talking about a big man, belittle him." We must develop the kind of contempt of American imperialism shown during the anti-American war in aid of Korea. Our principle is to learn all the strong points of other countries— in politics, economics, sciences, technology, literature, and arts.

Second, our revolution came late. Although the 1911 revolution which overthrew the monarchy preceded the Russian revolution, the victory of the people's revolution was achieved only in 1949, more than 30 years later than the October revolution. We cannot take pride in this. Of course, compared with some other colonial countries, our revolution is ahead of theirs. But here we must curb our conceit.

These two points are at once our weak and strong points. I have said before that we are very poor and not very knowledgeable. [We are] "poor and blank." Poverty means underdeveloped industries and agriculture; "blankness" is like the blankness of a piece of paper—a low standard of culture and science. Poverty [or an impasse] urged us to change, to revolt, and to search for strength. A piece of blank paper is just the thing for writing [or for making impressions on]. Of course I am speaking only in general terms. I do not imply that we are ignorant, in view of the wisdom of our laboring people and the existence of a contingent of good scientists.

Poverty and blankness have kept our tail down. Even if in future our industries are greatly expanded and our scientific and cultural standards greatly raised, we shall continue to be modest and considerate and refuse to stick our tail up. We shall keep on learning from others, for thousands of years to come. What is wrong with that?

In all, I have discussed ten points. To put it briefly, we must mobilize all the active, direct and indirect, and directly and indirectly active factors to struggle for the construction of a great socialist country. We must further strengthen and consolidate the socialist camp and fight for the victory of the international communist movement!

Internal Document. Not to be Lost. For study use, not to be quoted.

Printed by the "Toward the Sun" Brigade of education workers of the Economics Department, Peking College of Economics

December 22, 1966

Reprinted by the 303 Red Duplicating Unit at the Peking College of Economics

December 28, 1966

# 2

# War and Revolution

## THE AIM OF WAR (February 2, 1941)[1]

War, this monster of mutual slaughter among men, will be finally eliminated by the progress of human society, and in the not too distant future too. But there is only one way to eliminate it and that is to oppose war with war, to oppose counter-revolutionary war with revolutionary war, to oppose national counter-revolutionary war with national revolutionary war, to oppose counter-revolutionary class war with revolutionary class war. History knows only two kinds of war, revolutionary and counter-revolutionary. We support revolutionary wars and oppose counter-revolutionary wars. Only revolutionary wars are holy wars. We support the holy wars of national and class revolutions. The life of mankind is comprised of three eras—the era of peaceful life, the era of wartime life, and another era of peaceful life. We are now living in the transition from the second to the third era; the era of wartime life will be brought to an end by our own hands. The war we are conducting is unquestionably the last, and also the biggest and cruelest. The biggest and most ruthless of counter-revolutionary wars is hanging over us, and the vast majority of mankind will be destroyed unless we raise the banner of a revolutionary war. The banner of mankind's revolutionary war is the banner of mankind's salvation. The banner of China's revolutionary war is the banner of China's salvation. A war waged by the great majority of mankind and of the Chinese people is beyond doubt a holy war, a just war, a most lofty and glorious undertaking for the salvation of mankind and China, a bridge to a new era in world history, and a light-

---

[1] From "Problems of Strategy in China's Revolutionary War," *HC*, 1944 edition, supplement, pp. 113–14. See *SW*, I, 182–83.

86

house which shows the way to a new world.² Our study of the laws of revolutionary war springs from the desire to eliminate all wars.

### REVOLUTION (February 18, 1927)³

. . . a revolution is not a dinner party, or writing an essay, or painting a picture, or doing embroidery; it cannot be so refined, so leisurely and gentle, so temperate, kind, courteous, restrained and magnanimous. A revolution is an insurrection, an act of violence by which one class overthrows another. A rural revolution is a revolution by which the peasantry overthrows the power of the feudal landlord class. Without using the greatest force, the peasants cannot possibly overthrow the deep-rooted authority of the landlords which has lasted for thousands of years. The rural areas need a mighty revolutionary upsurge, for it alone can rouse the people in their millions to become a powerful force. . . . To put it bluntly, it is necessary to create terror for a while in every rural area, or otherwise it would be impossible to suppress the activities of the counter-revolutionaries in the countryside or overthrow the authority of the gentry. Proper limits have to be exceeded in order to right a wrong, or else the wrong cannot be righted.

### REVOLUTIONARY POTENTIALS OF THE PEASANTS (February 18, 1927)⁴

The peasants' revolt disturbed the gentry's sweet dreams. When the news from the countryside reached the cities, it caused immediate uproar among the gentry. Soon after my arrival in Changsha, I met all sorts of people and picked up a good deal of gossip. From the middle social strata upwards to the Kuomintang right-wingers, there was not a single person who did not sum up the whole business in the phrase, "It's terrible!" Under the impact of the views of the "It's terrible!" school then flooding the city, even quite revolutionary-minded people became down-hearted as they

² Literally, this sentence reads: "a lighthouse which turns the whole world into a new world."

³ From the *Guide Weekly*, No. 191, pp. 2063–64, or *SW*, I, 28–29.

⁴ From the *Guide Weekly*, No. 191, pp. 2062–63. See *SW*, I, 26–27

pictured the events in the countryside in their mind's eye; and they were unable to deny the word "terrible." Even quite progressive people said, "Though terrible, it is inevitable in a revolution." In short, nobody could altogether deny the word "terrible." But, as already mentioned, the fact is that the great peasant masses have risen to fulfill their historic mission and that the forces of rural democracy have risen to overthrow the forces of rural feudalism. To overthrow these feudal forces is the real objective of the national revolution. In a few months the peasants have accomplished what Dr. Sun Yat-sen wanted, but failed, to accomplish in the forty years he devoted to the national revolution. The patriarchal-feudal class of local tyrants, evil gentry and lawless landlords has formed the basis of autocratic government for thousands of years and is the corner-stone of imperialism, warlordism and corrupt officialdom. This is a marvellous feat never before achieved, not just in forty, but in thousands of years. It's fine. It is not "terrible" at all. It is anything but "terrible." If the merit in accomplishing the national revolution is to be rewarded, city dwellers and the military can claim no more than 30 percent of it whereas the peasants carrying on the revolution in the countryside should claim 70 percent. "It's terrible" is obviously a theory for combating the rise of the peasants in the interests of the landlords; it is obviously a theory of the landlord class for preserving the old order of feudalism and obstructing the establishment of the new order of democracy, it is obviously a counter-revolutionary theory. No revolutionary comrade should echo this nonsense. If your revolutionary viewpoint is firmly established and if you have been to the villages and looked around, you will undoubtedly feel thrilled as never before. Countless thousands of the enslaved—the peasants—are striking down the enemies who battened on their flesh. What the peasants are doing is absolutely right; what they are doing is fine! "It's fine!" is the theory of the peasants and of all other revolutionaries. Every revolutionary comrade should know that the national revolution requires a great change in the countryside. The Revolution of 1911 did not bring about this change, hence its failure. This change is now taking place, and it is an important factor for the completion of the revolution. Every revolutionary comrade must support it, or he is a counter-revolutionary.

# 3
## Mass Line

### THE POLITICAL CONSCIOUSNESS OF THE MASSES
(August 13, 1945)[1]

Apart from our own political consciousness, the political consciousness of the vanguard of the proletariat, there is the question of the political consciousness of the masses of the people. When the people are not yet politically conscious, it is entirely possible that their revolutionary gains may be handed over to others. This happened in the past. Today the level of political consciousness of the Chinese people is likewise very much higher. The prestige of our Party among the people has never been so great. Nevertheless, among the people, and chiefly among those living in the Japanese-occupied and Kuomintang areas, there are still a good many who believe in Chiang Kai-shek and have illusions about the Kuomintang and the United States of America, illusions which Chiang Kai-shek is working hard to spread. The fact that a section of the Chinese people is not yet politically conscious shows that much remains to be done in our propaganda and organizational work. The political awakening of the people is not easy. It requires much earnest effort on our part to rid their minds of wrong ideas. We should sweep backward ideas from the minds of the Chinese people, just as we sweep our rooms. Dust never vanishes of itself without sweeping. We must carry on extensive propaganda and education among the masses, so they will understand the real situation and trend in China and have confidence in their own strength.

[1] From "The Situation and Our Policy after the Victory in the War of Resistance against Japan," *HC*, IV, 1131, or *SW*, IV, 19.

### THE LEADERS AND THE LED (November 20, 1943)[2]

We Communists must be able to integrate ourselves with the masses in all things. If our Party members spend their whole lives sitting indoors and never go out to face the world and brave the storm, what good will they be to the Chinese people? None at all, and we do not need such people as Party members. We Communists ought to face the world and brave the storm, the great world of mass struggle and the mighty storm of mass struggle. "Three cobblers with their wits combined equal Chu-keh Liang the master mind." In other words, the masses have great creative power. In fact there are thousands upon thousands of Chu-keh Liangs among the Chinese people; every village, every town has its own. We should go to the masses and learn from them, synthesize their experience into better, articulated principles and methods, then do propaganda among the masses, and call upon them to put these principles and methods into practice so as to solve their problems and help them achieve liberation and happiness. If our comrades doing local work are isolated from the masses, fail to understand their feelings and to help them organize their production and improve their livelihood, and if they confine themselves to collecting "public grain for national salvation" without realizing that 10 percent of their energy is quite enough for this purpose provided they first devote 90 percent to helping the masses solve the problem of "private grain for the people's own salvation," then these comrades are contaminated with the Kuomintang style of work and covered with the dust of bureaucracy. The Kuomintang only demands things from the people and gives them nothing in return. If a member of our Party acts in this way, his style of work is that of the Kuomintang, and his face, caked with the dust of bureaucracy, needs a good wash in a basin of hot water. In my opinion, this bureaucratic style is to be found in local work in all our anti-Japanese base areas, and there are comrades who are isolated from the masses because they lack the mass viewpoint. We must firmly do away with this style of work before we can have close ties with the masses.

[2] From "Get Organized!" *HC*, III, 936, or *SW*, III, 158.

### MAO'S IDEAL ELITE (December 21,1939)[3]

Comrade [Norman] Bethune's spirit, his utter devotion to others without any thought of self, was shown in his great sense of responsibility in his work and his great warm-heartedness towards all comrades and the people. Every Communist must learn from him. There are not a few people who are irresponsible in their work, preferring the light and shirking the heavy, passing the burdensome tasks on to others and choosing the easy ones for themselves. At every turn they think of themselves before others. When they make some small contribution, they swell with pride and brag about it for fear that others will not know. They feel no warmth towards comrades and the people but are cold, indifferent and apathetic. In truth such people are not Communists, or at least cannot be counted as devoted Communists. No one who returned from the front failed to express admiration for Bethune whenever his name was mentioned, and none remained unmoved by his spirit. In the Shansi-Chahar-Hopei border area, no soldier or civilian was unmoved who had been treated by Dr. Bethune or had seen how he worked. Every Communist must learn this true communist spirit from Comrade Bethune.

### LEADERSHIP

#### A Talk at the General Report Conference, October 24, 1966 [4]

Chairman: "What's so terrifying? Have you seen Li Hsüeh-feng's[5] brief report? His two children went out and when they got back they started to educate their father—'Here's our old chief. Why are you so afraid of the Red Guards? We are not going to beat you up.' So he criticized himself. Wu Hsiu-ch'üan's[6] four chil-

---

[3] From "In Memory of Norman Bethune," *HC*, II, 653–54, or *SW*, II, 337–38.

[4] From *Mao Tse-tung ssu-hsiang wan-sui* (April, 1967), pp. 44–45.

[5] Li Hsüeh-feng became the First Secretary of the North China Bureau of the CCP in 1956 and succeeded P'eng Chen to the post of the First Secretary of the Party's Peking branch on June 3, 1966. See Donald W. Klein's article in the *China Quarterly*, No. 25 (January–March, 1966), pp. 222–23.

[6] Wu Hsiu-ch'üan, a member of the Central Committee of the CCP and an important official in the Ministry of Foreign Affairs, became famous for his par-

dren were divided into four factions. Many of their schoolmates went
to see them, sometimes as many as a dozen. Since Wu came into
contact with a lot of them, he didn't feel scared. On the contrary,
he thought they were rather likeable. If you want to educate others,
you must educate yourself to begin with. These people, they are
incoherent, daren't see the Red Guards, don't speak truthfully with
the students, and are bureaucrats. At first they avoided [the Red
Guards]; [when they come face to face with the Red Guards] they
daren't speak up. Years of revolution have made them more stupid
than ever. [Liu] Shao-ch'i wrote to Chiang Wei-ch'ing,[7] criticizing
him and saying how silly Chiang was. But is Liu clever?"

Chairman asked Liu Lan-t'ao:[8] "What are you going to do when
you get back?" Liu replied: "I'll see when I get back." Chairman
remarked: "You always equivocate, don't you?"

Chairman asked the Premier[9] about the Conference and the
Premier said: "It's mostly done. Tomorrow there will be half a
day's meeting. As to the concrete problems, they will be dealt with
according to the principles [agreed upon at the Conference] when
they return." Chairman asked Li Ching-ch'üan:[10] "How about Liao
Chih-kao?"[11] Li answered: "He was confused at the beginning, but
showed improvement as the Conference progressed." Chairman
said: "Who's consistently right? You yourself slipped away, and
were frightened out of your wits, and went to stay in the military
district [of Ch'engtu]. When you return, you'd better pull up your
socks and do better. It's no good to stick up Liu's and Teng's big-
character posters in the main streets. [You] must make allowances
for other people's mistakes and let them get on with the revolution.

---

ticipation in the UN Security Council's discussion on the Korean War on December 16, 1950.

[7] Chiang Wei-ch'ing was the First Secretary of the CCP Chekiang branch and
has been under attack as one of the "handful of capitalist roaders." The *People's
Daily*, April 12, 1968, and BBC *Summary of World Broadcasts*, FE/2754/B5–6.

[8] Liu Lan-t'ao was the First Secretary of the Northwest Bureau of the CCP.
See D. W. Klein's article in the *China Quarterly*, No. 271, pp. 223–24.

[9] Refers to Chou En-lai.

[10] Li Ching-ch'üan was born in Huich'ang, Kiangsi, in 1907. He was a member of the Politburo and the First Secretary of the Southwest Bureau of the
CCP before his dismissal on July 5, 1967 by the issue of the "Ten Red Articles."

[11] Liao Chih-kao was the First Secretary of the Szechwan branch of the CCP
and has been branded as a "capitalist roader." BBC *Summary of World Broadcasts*, FE/2745/B11–17.

Will you promise to mend your ways? Let the Red Guards read *The True Story of Ah Q.*" . . .

Chairman asked Li Hsien-nien:[12] "How's the Conference today?" Li replied: "The College of Finance and Economics said that they were going to hold a criticism meeting tomorrow. I made it clear that I would criticize myself, but they didn't allow me to speak." Chairman said: "Are you going to be criticized tomorrow? You will run away before they open their mouths." Li said: "I'll go abroad tomorrow." Chairman commented: "You'd better tell them that in the past it was the mother who taught her son; now it's the son who teaches his mother. I think you lack a bit of spirit. Even if they don't listen to your self-criticism, you should still criticize yourself. If they criticize you, you should admit your mistakes. The chaos was created by the Center and both the Center and the regions should be responsible. My responsibility was the division of two lines. Why did I do it? First, because . . . , and second, because of the experience of the Soviet Union. Malenkov was immature, having no power when Stalin was alive. He drank toasts and said nice things all right. So I thought I'd establish their [the comrades' on the first line] prestige before I died. I didn't expect the contrary to happen." T'ao Chu[13] added: "The great power fell [into the hands of those] beside you."

Chairman went on: "This was purposely done. But now it has developed into independent kingdoms. On many things, I wasn't even consulted. For instance, the land conference, the Tientsin talk, the Shansi co-operatives, the abolition of investigation and research, and the eulogy of Wang Kuang-mei.[14] All these things could have

[12] Li Hsien-nien was born in Huangan, Hupei, in 1905 and is a vice premier concurrently in charge of the Ministry of Finance.

[13] T'ao Chu, a Hunanese, was born in 1904. In 1925, he was at the Whampoa Military Academy with Lin Piao and Lo Jui-ch'ing. He made his mark in the Korean War in 1951, when he was in charge of army supplies. In 1952, he became the First Secretary of the South China Bureau, whence he was promoted to the First Secretaryship of the Central-South Bureau in 1961. He was made a vice premier in January, 1965, the head of the Propaganda Department of the CCP in July, 1966, and a member of the Politburo in September, 1966. His fall in January was soon followed by a public criticism meeting of him at the Peking Stadium on February 25, 1967. See D. W. Klein's article in the *China Quarterly*, No. 23 (July–September, 1965), pp. 65–66.

[14] This may refer to the land conference held in September, 1947, when the Center of the Party was separated into two groups, and Mao was not with the

properly been done through a discussion at the party Center. But
Teng Hsiao-p'ing never paid me a visit. He did not consult me on
anything since 1959. In 1962 suddenly four vice-Premiers came to
Nanking to see me. They were Li Fu-ch'un, T'an Chen-lin, Li
Hsien-nien, and Po I-po. Then they went to Tientsin. I immediately promised them [what they asked for] before they went back
[to Peking]. Still Teng Hsiao-p'ing didn't come. I was dissatisfied
with the Wuch'ang conference;[15] the high targets were utterly impossible. Then there was the Peking conference.[16] You had held meetings for six days. I asked for one more day but it couldn't be done.
To have failed to fulfill your tasks wasn't as bad as to have lost your
parents! After the Tsunyi conference,[17] the Center was more centralized. But after the sixth plenum of 1938, Hsiang Ying and P'eng
Teh-huai (the New Fourth Army Incident in south Anhwei and
the Hundred Regiment Campaign of P'eng Chen[18]) developed their
independent kingdoms. They didn't even bother to tell me. After
the Seventh Congress, there was not even a single man in the Center.

---

majority group. See Jen Pi-shih's article in the *T'u-kai cheng-tang tien-hsing
ching-nien* [Exemplary experiences of land reform and party reform] (Hong
Kong, 1948), p. 41.

The Tientsin talks were given by Liu Shao-ch'i to the business circles of the
city in the spring of 1950; see *Ming Pao Monthly* (Hong Kong), No. 14, p. 30.
"The Trials of Wang Kuang-mei," issued in the *Current Background* by the
American Consulate in Hong Kong, No. 848 (February 27, 1968), p. 11 also refers to these talks.

The Shansi co-operatives are referred to in Liu Shao-ch'i's alleged self-
examination. See also the *Hsin-hua yüeh-pao* [New China Monthly], June, 1952,
pp. 106ff.

The praise of Wang Kuang-mei was concerned mainly with her activities in
the T'aoyuan commune and Tsinghua University. See the *Current Background*,
No. 848 (February 27, 1968).

[15] The conference was held on December 1, 1958.

[16] The Peking conference was held in June, 1964.

[17] The Tsunyi conference was held on January 8, 1935. It is quite wrong
to say that the conference took place January 1–3, because the Communist
troops did not take the city until the 7th. See Jerome Ch'en, *Mao and the
Chinese Revolution*, pp. 188–90.

[18] Ch'en, *Mao and the Chinese Revolution*, pp. 251–52, 246. Hsiang Ying was
the political commissar of the New Fourth Army. About P'eng Teh-huai's role
in the Hundred Regiment Campaign, see also the Red Guard newspaper translated in the *Survey of China Mainland Press*, No. 4047 (October 25, 1967), p. 9.
The reference to P'eng Chen in the text may be a misprint.

When Hu Tsung-nan entered Yenan,[19] the Center was divided into two—1 with [Chou] En-lai and Jen Pi-shih in north Shensi and Liu Shao-ch'i with Chu Teh in the northeast. The Center was still somewhat centralized. Once we entered the cities,[20] we dispersed, huddling in small groups. There came even more dispersal after the division of the 1st and 2nd lines. After the finance and economics conference of 1953 I told them to communicate with each other—with the Center and with the regions. Liu and Teng have always done their work in the open, unlike P'eng Chen. Previously, Ch'en Tu-hsiu, Chang Kuo-t'ao, Wang Ming, Lo Chang-lung, and Li Li-san had all done their work in the open. That wasn't serious. Kao Kang, Jao Shu-shih, and P'eng Teh-huai were double-dealers and P'eng was in league with them. I knew nothing about this. P'eng Chen, Lo Jui-ch'ing, Lu Ting-yi, and Yang Shang-k'un had done their work in secret and secrecy never does anyone any good. Those who followed mistaken lines must correct themselves. Ch'en [Tu-hsiu], Wang [Ming], and Li [Li-san] didn't do that . . . (Chou En-lai interrupted: "Li Li-san didn't rectify his thought. No matter what small cliques, the thing to do is to block it air-tight. What is needed is to unify our thought in order to achieve unity. [We] must allow Liu and Teng to join the revolution and correct themselves. You may say that I am clowning. So I am.") At the Seventh Congress, Ch'en X [Yün?] said: "Don't elect anyone of the Wang Ming line to the Central Committee," but Wang Ming and several others were in fact elected to the committee. Now only Wang Ming has dropped out; who else? Lo-fu [Chang Wen-t'ien] [21] was no good; Wang Chia-hsiang I rather liked, for he supported the battle of Tungkang.[22] At the Ningtu conference,[23] Lo-fu wanted to expel me [from the party], but Chou [En-lai] and Chu [Teh] objected. At the Tsunyi conference he [Chang Wen-t'ien] played a useful

---

[19] Jerome Ch'en, *op. cit.*, pp. 282–83.

[20] This refers to the 1949 victory (*SW*, IV, 337–39).

[21] Chang Wen-t'ien, see above, p. 15. About his downfall see a Red Guard newspaper translated in the *Survey of China Mainland Press*, No. 4047 (October 25, 1967), p. 7.

[22] Tungkang may be a misprint of Lungkang. The battle of Lungkang took place in April, 1934. See General Hsüeh Yüeh, *Chiao-fei chi-shih* [A veritable account of the anti-bandit campaigns] (Taipei, 1962), pp. 18ff., 23.

[23] Jerome Ch'en, *op. cit.*, p. 176.

role. It was impossible then without them [the 28 Bolsheviks]. But Lo-fu was stubborn. [Liu] Shao-ch'i and Nieh Jung-chen were against them. We must not get rid of Liu Shao-ch'i by a stroke of the pen. They [Liu and others] have committed mistakes, but let them correct themselves!

### A Talk at the Work Conference of the Center, October 25, 1966 [24]

Let me say a few words. Two points. For 17 years now, one thing, I think, has been done badly. For considerations for the security of the country and in view of Stalin's experience, two lines [of leadership] were arranged—I was on the second line and other comrades on the first. Now I can see that it wasn't ideal, too dispersed. Once [we] got into the cities, [we] lost centralization. There were a lot of independent kingdoms. This was changed at the 11th plenum. This is the first point. I was on the second line; I didn't take charge of the daily routine. Many things were done by others in the hope that this might increase their prestige, so that when I go to see God the country won't receive such a shock [as it may otherwise]. Everyone agreed with me on this. It seems that the comrades on the first line haven't done their work well and some of the things they ought to have done were left undone. The blame, however, is not entirely theirs; I am also responsible. Why do I say that I am also responsible? First, to divide the Standing Committee [of the Politburo] into the first and second lines and to let them take charge of the Secretariat was my idea. Furthermore, [I] had too much trust in them. I became aware of this at the time of the 23 Points.[25] Then Peking couldn't do a thing; nor could the Center. It was in September or October last year when this question was raised: If there was revisionism in the Center, what would the regions do about it? I felt that my views couldn't be accepted in

---

[24] From *Mao Tse-tung ssu-hsiang wan-sui* (April, 1967), p. 40.

[25] "Some current problems arising in the course of rural socialist education movement," adopted by the Work Conference of the Politburo, January 14, 1965, published by the CCP Fukien Provincial Publishing House, January 18, 1965. See also C. Neuhauser's article in the *China Quarterly*, No. 32.

Peking. Why wasn't the criticism of Wu Han[26] started in Peking but in Shanghai? This was because there were no available men in Peking. Now the question of Peking is solved.

[26] Wu Han was born in Iwu, Chekiang in 1909 and took his first degree at the Tsinghua University. His scholarship attracted the attention of Dr. Hu Shih and from 1937 to 1946, he was on the staff of the Department of History of the Southwest Associated University, Kunming. From 1946 to 1948, he was at the Tsinghua University in Peking whence with the help of Li Wei-han and Liu Jen he fled to the Communist-controlled areas on the eve of the 1949 victory. He became the vice-mayor of Peking in 1949. Yao Wen-yuan's attack on his play, the *Dismissal of Hai Jui,* was published on November 10, 1965.

# 4
# Intellectual Life

## A Letter Written after Mao's Second Visit to Peking

Indeed, it is important to have a good and infectious morale. The old atmosphere of China is too heavy and suffocating. We certainly need a new, powerful atmosphere in order to be able to change it. We must have a group of *people*, fearless of hardships and strong willed for the creation of this new atmosphere; what we need more is commonly accepted political philosophy (*chu-i*). No new atmosphere can be created without such a political philosophy. I think our Society [the New Citizens' Study Society—tr.] must not remain merely a gathering of men based on personal feelings, but rather it should be transformed into an association based on a political philosophy. A political philosophy is like a banner which gives us hope and a sense of direction, once it is hoisted.

## IDEOLOGY AND CULTURE (1940)[2]

A given culture is the ideological reflection of the politics and economics of a given society. There is in China an imperialist culture which is a reflection of imperialist rule, or partial rule, in the political and economic fields. This culture is fostered not only by the cultural organizations run directly by the imperialists in China but by a number of Chinese who have lost all sense of shame. Into this category falls all culture which reflects her semi-feudal politics and economy, and whose exponents include all those who

[1] From *Hsin-min Hsüeh-hui hui-yüan t'ung-hsun-chi* [Correspondence of the members of the New Citizens' Study Society], *Hunan li-shih tzu-liao*, No. 4 (1949), p. 76.
[2] From "On New Democracy," January, 1940, *SW*, II, 369–70.

advocate the worship of Confucius, the study of the Confucian canon, the old ethical code and the old ideas in opposition to the new culture and new ideas. Imperialist culture and semi-feudal culture are devoted brothers and have formed a reactionary cultural alliance against China's new culture. This kind of reactionary cultural alliance serves the imperialists and the feudal class and must be swept away. Unless it is swept away, no new culture of any kind can be built up. There is no construction without destruction, no flowing without damming and no motion without rest; the two are locked in a life-and-death struggle.

As for the new culture, it is the ideological reflection of the new politics and the new economy which it sets out to serve.

### NEW-DEMOCRATIC CULTURE [3]

New-democratic culture is national. It opposes imperialist oppression and upholds the dignity and independence of the Chinese nation. It belongs to our own nation and bears our own national characteristics. It links up with the socialist and new-democratic cultures of all other nations and they are related in such a way that they can absorb something from each other and help each other to develop, together forming a new world culture; but as a revolutionary national culture it can never link up with any reactionary imperialist culture of whatever nation. To nourish her own culture, China needs to assimilate a good deal of foreign progressive culture, not enough of which was done in the past. We should assimilate whatever is useful to us today not only from the present-day socialist and new-democratic cultures but also from the earlier cultures of other nations, for example, from the culture of the various capitalist countries in the Age of Enlightenment. However, we should not gulp any of this foreign material down uncritically, but must treat it as we do our food—first chewing it, then submitting it to the working of the stomach and intestines with their juices and secretions, and separating it into nutrient to be absorbed and waste matter to be discarded—before it can nourish us. To advocate "wholesale westernization" is wrong. China has suffered a great deal from the mechanical absorption of foreign material. Similarly,

[3] From "On New Democracy," January, 1940, *SW*, II, 380–82.

in applying Marxism to China, Chinese communists must fully and properly integrate the universal truth of Marxism with the concrete practice of the Chinese revolution, or in other words, the universal truth of Marxism must be combined with specific national characteristics and acquire a definite national form if it is to be useful, and in no circumstances can it be applied subjectively as a mere formula. Marxists who make a fetish of formulas are simply playing the fool with Marxism and the Chinese revolution, and there is no room for them in the ranks of the Chinese revolution. Chinese culture should have its own form, its own national form. National in form and new-democratic in content—such is our new culture today.

New-democratic culture is scientific. Opposed as it is to all feudal and superstitious ideas, it stands for seeking truth from facts, for objective truth and for the unity of theory and practice. On this point, the possibility exists of a united front against imperialism, feudalism, and superstition between the scientific thought of the Chinese proletariat and those Chinese bourgeois materialists and natural scientists who are progressive, but in no case is there a possibility of a united front with any reactionary idealism. In the field of political action Communists may form an anti-imperialist and anti-feudal united front with some idealists and even religious people, but we can never approve of their idealism or religious doctrines. A splendid old culture was created during the long period of Chinese feudal society. To study the development of this old culture, to reject its feudal dross and assimilate its democratic essence is a necessary condition for developing our new national culture and increasing our national self-confidence, but we should never swallow anything and everything uncritically. It is imperative to separate the fine old culture of the people which had a more or less democratic and revolutionary character from all the decadence of the old feudal ruling class. China's present new politics and new economy have developed out of her old politics and old economy, and her present new culture, too, has developed out of her old culture; therefore, we must respect our own history and must not lop it off. However, respect for history means giving it its proper place  as a science, respecting its dialectical development, and not eulogizing the past at the expense of the present or praising every drop of feudal poison. As far as the masses and the young students are concerned, the essential thing is to guide them to look forward and not backward.

New-democratic culture belongs to the broad masses and is there-fore democratic. It should serve the toiling masses of workers and peasants who make up more than 90 percent of the nation's popula-tion and should gradually become their very own. There is a differ-ence of degree, as well as a close link, between the knowledge im-parted to the revolutionary cadres and the knowledge imparted to the revolutionary masses, between the raising of cultural standards and popularization. Revolutionary culture is a powerful revolution-ary weapon for the broad masses of the people. It prepares the ground ideologically before the revolution comes and is an import-ant, indeed essential, fighting front in the general revolutionary front during the revolution. People engaged in revolutionary cul-tural work are the commanders at various levels on this cultural front. . . . A revolutionary cultural worker who is not close to the people is a commander without an army, whose fire-power cannot bring the enemy down. . . .

A national, scientific and mass culture—such is the anti-im-perialist and anti-feudal culture of the people, the culture of New Democracy, the new culture of the Chinese nation.

## BOOKISH KNOWLEDGE AND PRACTICE (February 1, 1942)[4]

How can those who have only book-learning be turned into intellectuals in the true sense? The only way is to get them to take part in practical work and become practical workers, to get those engaged in theoretical work to study important practical problems. In these ways our aim can be attained.

What I have said will probably make some people angry. They will say, "According to your explanation, even Marx would not be regarded as an intellectual." I say they are wrong. Marx took part in the revolutionary movement and also created revolutionary theory. Beginning with the commodity, the simplest element of capitalism, he made a thorough study of the economic structure of

[4] From "Rectify the Party's Style of Work," *HC*, III, 818–20, or *SW*, III, 40–41.

capitalist society. Millions of people saw and handled commodities every day but were so used to them that they took no notice. Marx alone studied commodities scientifically. He carried out a tremendous work of research into their actual development and derived a thoroughly scientific theory from what existed universally. He studied nature, history and proletarian revolution and created dialectical materialism, historical materialism and the theory of proletarian revolution. Thus Marx became a most completely developed intellectual, representing the acme of human wisdom; he was fundamentally different from those who have only book-learning. Marx undertook detailed investigations and studies in the course of practical struggles, formed generalizations and then verified his conclusions by testing them in practical struggles—this is what we call theoretical work. Our Party needs a large number of comrades who will learn how to do such work. In our Party there are many comrades who can learn to do this kind of theoretical research; most of them are intelligent and promising and we should value them. But they must follow correct principles and not repeat the mistake of the past. They must discard dogmatism and not confine themselves to ready-made phrases in books.

There is only one kind of true theory in this world, theory that is drawn from objective reality and then verified by objective reality; nothing else is worthy of the name of theory in our sense. Stalin said that theory becomes aimless when it is not connected with practice. Aimless theory is useless and false and should be discarded. We should point the finger of scorn at those who are fond of aimless theorizing. Marxism-Leninism is the most correct, scientific and revolutionary truth, born out of and verified by objective reality, but many who study Marxism-Leninism take it as lifeless dogma, thus impeding the development of theory and harming themselves as well as other comrades.

On the other hand, our comrades who are engaged in practical work will also come to grief if they misuse their experience. True, these people are often rich in experience, which is very valuable, but it is very dangerous if they rest content with their own experience. They must realize that their knowledge is mostly perceptual and partial and that they lack rational and comprehensive knowledge; in other words, they lack theory and their knowledge, too, is relatively incomplete. Without comparatively complete knowledge it is impossible to do revolutionary work well.

Thus, there are two kinds of incomplete knowledge, one is ready-made knowledge found in books and the other is knowledge that is mostly perceptual and partial; both are one-sided. Only an integration of the two can yield knowledge that is sound and relatively complete.

## A TALK IN HANGCHOW (December 21, 1965)[5]

I have read three articles in the current issue of the *Che-hsüeh yen-chiu* (philosophical studies). When you write on philosophy, you must write on practical philosophy if you want people to read [what you write]. Who wants to read abstruse, bookish philosophy? Some intellectuals, like Wu Han[6] and Chien Po-tsan,[7] are getting worse and worse. Now there is a man called Sun Ta-jen[8] who has specially written to refute what Chien Po-tsan calls the "concession" the feudal landlords made to the peasants. After a peasant war, the landlord class only counterattacked and went back to the *status quo ante* (lit. re-settled accounts in their favor); there was no such thing as "concession." The landlord class did not make any concession to the T'aip'ing Heavenly Kingdom.[9] The Boxers[10] raised the slogan "Rebel against the Ch'ing and wipe out the foreigners" to begin with, and then [changed to] "Suppress the Ch'ing and wipe out the foreigners"; therefore they got the support from Tz'u-hsi.[11] The Ch'ing was defeated by the imperialists; Tz'u-hsi and Kuang-hsü[12] fled. She began to "support

[5] From *Mao Tse-tung ssu-hsiang wan-sui* (April, 1967), pp. 31–34.

[6] Wu Han, see above, p. 97, *n.*

[7] Chien Po-tsan, an eminent historian who has been subject to severe criticism since the Cultural Revolution.

[8] The translator is unable to find any information about this man.

[9] The T'aip'ing Rebellion (1850–64), inspired by a kind of Christianity, was one of the greatest rebellions in Chinese history; it nearly toppled the Ch'ing dynasty.

[10] The Boxer uprising (1898–1900) changed its political line from anti-dynastic to pro-dynastic, but remained anti-foreign throughout the movement.

[11] Tz'u-hsi, the Dowager Empress (1835–1908), who acquired a great deal of state power from 1861 onwards and became one of the most important political figures until her death.

[12] Kuang-hsü (1871–1908) reigned from 1875 to 1908 and thus was constantly

the foreigners and wipe out the Boxers." Some people say that the
*Secret History of the Ch'ing Court*[13] is a patriotic play. I think it
is treacherous, through and through. Why do some people say that
it is patriotic? The reasons are no more than that the emperor,
Kuang-hsü, was pitiable and he and K'ang Yu-wei[14] had set up
some schools, organized a new army,[15] and adopted some other
enlightened measures.

At the end of the Ch'ing dynasty, some people advocated "Chinese learning as the essence and western learning for application." [16] The "essence," something similar to our general line, could
not be changed. Since it was impossible to use the "essence" of
western learning, of a democratic republic, of the "natural rights
of men" (*t'ien-fu jen-ch'uan,* lit. people's rights given by heaven)
or of "the theory of evolution" (*t'ien-yen lun,* lit. the theory of the
evolvement of heaven), the only thing applicable was western technology. Of course, "people's rights given by heaven" is a wrong
theory. What are "people's rights given by heaven"? "People's
rights" are given by "the people" themselves. Are our rights, the
people's rights, given by heaven? Our rights are given by the people
(*lao pai-hsing*), primarily by the working class and the poor and
lower middle peasants.

A study of [our] modern history will show that there was no such
thing as "concession"; there were only concessions made by the
revolutionary forces to the reactionaries while the latter always
counterattacked and tried to restore the *status quo ante.* Each time
when a new dynasty appeared in history, a tax reduction policy
was adopted because the people were so poor that there was nothing

---

under the shadow of the Dowager Empress. He was the sovereign responsible
for the short-lived Reform of 1898.

[13] "The Secret History of the Ch'ing Court" was written by Yao K'e and made
into a film in Hong Kong in 1948. After 1949, it became the center of a controversy among Chinese film and literary critics. The controversy was revived as
a part of the political struggle in the Cultural Revolution.

[14] K'ang Yu-wei (1858–1927) was the central figure of the 1898 Reform.

[15] The Newly Created Army was trained by Yuan Shih-k'ai in 1896.

[16] Having adopted this cultural attitude in 1860, Chinese scholars and officials
eventually coined this phrase after the Sino-Japanese war of 1895. See J. Leven-
son, *Confucian China and Its Modern Fate: the Problem of Intellectual Con-
tinuity* (Berkeley, Calif., 1958), Part III, Ch. iv.

to be taken away [from them]. The tax reduction policy was [in fact] advantageous to the landlord class.

[I hope] philosophers will go to stay in a factory or a village for a few years. [I hope] they will change their system of philosophy, write in a different way, and write less.

There is a student in Nanking University, a history student from a peasant family. He has taken part in the "four pure movement" [17] and written some articles urging historians to go to the countryside. His articles have been published in the University magazine. He has also confessed (tzu-pai): "I have studied several years and there is not a trace of manual labor in my mind." In the same issue of the University magazine there is another article which says: "Substance is the principal contradiction (principal contradictions are contained in substance)." I have not said anything like this. Phenomena are what one can see which stimulate one's sense [of sight]; substance [however] cannot be seen or touched. Hiding behind phenomena, substance can be discovered only after investigation and research. If substance could be seen or touched, then there would be no need of science.

[We] must step by step come into contact with reality, to work in a village for a few years, and study agricultural sciences on plants, soil, fertilizers, bacteria, forests, and water conservancy. [We] do not have to open big tomes or small pamphlets; a bit of commonsense will do.

This university education of ours! We suspect that from primary to university education, altogether in 16, 17, or 20 years, [the students do not even have a chance] to see rice, peas, wheat, cereals, and millet. They do not see how workers work, how peasants plough, and how business is done. [Only] their health is ruined. It is really like murder. I have told my children: "Go to the countryside and tell the poor and lower middle peasants. Tell them that your father said: 'The more we learn, the more stupid we become. Uncles, brothers, and sisters, we have come to learn from you.' " In fact, a child before he goes to school at seven has had wide contact with society. At two he begins to learn to speak; at

[17] This refers to the purification of politics, thought, organization, and economy—a movement started in 1964 to herald the coming of the Cultural Revolution.

three he quarrels loudly with others; later he picks up a small hoe and hoes the land imitating the adults. This is the objective world. He has also learned concepts—"dog" is a larger concept whereas "black and yellow dogs" is a more limited concept. The yellow dog at his home is a real thing. Man is a concept which has many things (special qualities) stripped from it, such as male and female, adult and young, Chinese and foreign, and revolutionary and reactionary. What is left [in the concept of man] is that man is not beast. Who has seen man? One can only see Chang the third or Li the fourth. "House" is another concept which no one can see. One can see only a concrete house—a foreign-style house in Tientsin or a compound in Peking.

University education must be reformed. Class hours should be shortened. The faculties of arts in particular have to be reformed. As they are, can they produce philosophers, men of letters, or historians? Nowadays philosophers do not work on philosophy; men of letters do not write novels; historians do not work on history, only on emperors, kings, generals, and ministers. Ch'i Pen-yü's[18] (e.g. "Study history for revolution") is excellent, but it does not name names; Yao Wen-yuan's[19] ("A criticism of the new historical opera, the *Dismissal of Hai Jui*") does name names, but it fails to hit where it really hurts.

All university arts faculties have to be reformed. Their students should work in industries, agriculture, and commerce. Science and engineering faculties are different. They have their practice workshops and laboratories. They do their work and experiments there. After graduation from a senior middle school, a student should do

[18] Ch'i made his name by his essay on the role of Li Hsiu-ch'eng in the T'aip'ing Rebellion. The essay drew Chiang Ch'ing's (Mme. Mao Tse-tung) attention and, through Chiang Ch'ing, Mao's attention. This accounted for his rise to power and his inclusion in the Central Cultural Revolution Team under Ch'en Po-ta. Early in 1968, he was accused of uncontrolled personal ambitions and of collecting "black material" on such mighty figures as Lin Piao and Chou En-lai. He is now in disgrace.

[19] Yao Wen-yuan is the son of Yao P'eng-tzu, a left-wing writer of the 1930's. It was when the "Hundred Flowers Campaign" turned into the antirightist campaign in 1957–8 that he caught the tide of events and became famous. His vehement attack on Wu Han signaled the beginning of the Cultural Revolution. Since then, he has brought down such a powerful leader as T'ao Chu of south China. He is now on the Central Cultural Revolution Team under Ch'en Po-ta.

some practical work. Village work alone is not enough; he should also work in a factory, a shop, and an army company. After a few years' work like this, he need no more than two more years' study. Let us say five years' work down below. Teachers should go down [to do practical work] too. They can work and teach at the same time. Can philosophy, literature, and history not be taught down below? Must they be taught in tall, foreign-style buildings?

The great inventors [James] Watt and [Thomas] Edison began their careers as workers; the discoverer of electricity [Benjamin] Franklin sold newspapers, was a newspaper boy. Many great scholars and scientists in the past were not graduates of universities, and many comrades in our party Center are not graduates either.

The present way of writing books ought to be changed. Take analysis and synthesis for instance. They have not been explained clearly. Some books say: "Synthesis is contained in analysis," and "analysis and synthesis are inseparable." These may be true, but not complete. The books should also say that analysis and synthesis are both separable and inseparable. Everything is separable: One can always be split into two.

Analysis depends on the conditions [under which it is done]. Take the analysis of the KMT and CCP for instance. How did we analyze the KMT? We said that it controlled a large area, many people, and big cities. It had the support of the imperialists. It had a large and well equipped army. But the fundamental thing was that it was not with the masses, the peasants and soldiers. It had its internal contradictions. Our army was smaller and poorly equipped (millet plus rifles). We controlled less land and no big cities. We had no foreign aid. But we were with the masses, had the three great democracies, and established the three-eight style.[20] We represented the wishes of the people—this was the fundamental thing.

Of the KMT officers, those who had graduated from the Army University[21] could not fight but those who had gone through a few

[20] The "Three-eight style" is based on *three* phrases and *eight* characters selected by Mao for the training of the Army. They are: firm, correct political orientation; plain, hard-working style; and flexibility in strategy and tactics; and unity, alertness, earnestness, and liveliness.

[21] The War College set up by the Peking Government in the 1910's was one of the earliest and the highest military academies of China.

months' training at the Whampoa Military Academy[22] could. Very few of our marshals and generals are graduates from universities. I did not read any book on strategy either. I read *Tso's Commentary, The Mirror for Administration,* and *The Romance of the Three Kingdoms*[23] which recorded how battles were fought. But they did not influence me when I was actually fighting. When we fought, we did not take any book with us. We just analyzed the war situation between ourselves and the enemy, the concrete situation.

To synthesize means to eat up the enemy. How did we synthesize the KMT? It was no more than to take over whatever belonged to our enemy and reform it. We did not kill the captured soldiers— some were released and others absorbed into our ranks. We took [their] arms, food, and equipment. What we did not want, to use a philosophical term, we negated, such as people like Tu Yü-ming.[24] Eating has its analysis and synthesis, too. Eating crabs for example. One eats only the meat, not the shell. The stomach and intestines absorb what is nutritious and get rid of the rubbish. Yours is foreign philosophy; mine is native. To synthesize the KMT is to eat it up— absorbing most of it and getting rid of a small part of it. This is learned from Marx who absorbed the valuable kernel but rejected the shell of Hegel's philosophy, to formulate his materialist dialectics. He took materialism from [Ludwig] Feuerbach but criticized Feuerbach's metaphysics. What should be inherited was [or is to be] inherited. Marx absorbed what was good and rejected what was bad in French utopian socialism and English political economy.

In his *Capital,* Marx analyzes the beginning of the dual character

[22] The Whampoa Military Academy was set up by the Kuomintang with Russian help at Whampoa, near Canton, in 1924. Chiang Kai-shek was appointed its Commandant. After the Northern Expedition it was moved to Nanking to become the Central Military Academy.

[23] Tso Ch'iu-ming's commentary on the *Spring and Autumn Annals* was a classic on ancient Chinese history; *Tzu-chih t'ung-chien* [The Mirror for Administration] was a general history compiled by Ssu-ma Kuang of the Sung dynasty; and *The Romance of the Three Kingdoms,* a historical novel based on the *Chronicles of the Three Kingdoms* (A.D. 220–65), was written by Lo Kuan-chung of the Ming dynasty.

[24] The Kuomintang general who commanded the decisive battle of Huai-Hai at the end of 1948 and the beginning of 1949. After the defeat, he was captured by the Communists.

of the commodity. Our commodities also have a dual character. The commodities a hundred years later will have a dual character, too. Our comrades [for example] have theirs—their right and wrong. Do you have your dual character? I do. Young people are likely to be influenced by metaphysics: No one dares to point out their weaknesses. They improve as they have more experience. In recent years, the young people have showed progress. However, it is difficult to deal with old professors. Wu Han is the [vice] mayor [of Peking]. Perhaps he would do better as a magistrate [of a county]. Yang Hsien-chen and Chang Wen-t'ien[25] are also better demoted. That may be a good way to help them.

Recently there were people writing on the law of full justification. What is the law of full justification? I do not think it exists. Different classes have different justifications. Which one of them has not got its full justification? Does [Bertrand] Russell have his justification? He sent me a pamphlet of his which ought to be translated and read. Politically, Russell has shown progress. He is anti-revisionist and anti-American. He is supporting [North] Vietnam. This idealist is a bit materialistic now. [I am] referring to his activities.

One should do all sorts of work and make contacts with all sorts of people. A leftist must not be with other leftists all the time; he ought to be with the rightists too. Do not be afraid of this and that. I, for example, have seen all kinds of people, big officials and small officials, and the rest.

Can the style of philosophical writings be altered somewhat? Write them in a popular style, in the language of the working people. We all write in the manner of a student. (Interruption from Comrade Ch'en Po-ta:[26] "Except the Chairman.") I have done work

[25] Yang Hsien-chen, a member of the Central Committee of the CCP, was a teacher in philosophy at the Higher Party School. In 1964, his theory of "combining two into one" (hence the negation of contradictions) was harshly criticized. See D. Munro, "The Yang Hsien-chen Affair," the *China Quarterly*, No. 22 (April–June, 1965).

[26] Now a member of the Politburo, Ch'en is believed to be Mao's secretary for many years. He was a champion of the Mao cult shortly before the Rectification Campaign of 1942 and has published pamphlets and articles on Chinese history and philosophy. He is at present the leader of the Central Cultural Revolution Team.

in the peasant movement, labor movement, student movement, and the KMT movement. I have done military work for more than twenty years. That is why I am slightly better.

In philosophical research, [one] should study Chinese history and the historical development of Chinese philosophies, beginning with the history of the past hundred years. Is historical development a unification of contradictions? Modern history is a continuous process of one being split into two, of incessant struggles. In the struggles, some made compromises. But these did not satisfy the people who wanted to fight on. Before the 1911 revolution, Sun Yat-sen and K'ang Yu-wei had to fight each other. After it, after the overthrow of the emperor, Sun and Yuan Shih-k'ai[27] struggled against each other. Then the KMT bred its own dissensions and struggles one after the other.

One should write prefaces[28] and annotations to the classics of Marxism-Leninism [when one reads them]. It is easier to write a political than a philosophical preface to them. It was said that dialectics had three basic laws and then Stalin said that there were four. But I think there is only one basic law—the law of contradictions. Quality and quantity, affirmation and negation, substance and phenomenon, content and form, inevitability and freedom, possibility and reality, and etc. are unifications of contradictions.

It is said that formal logic is to dialectics as elementary arithmetic is to advanced mathematics. This statement needs further study. Formal logic deals with the form of thinking; it says that what goes before does not contradict what comes after. It is a special branch of science needed for all writing.

Formal logic does not consider, and is incapable of considering, major premises. The KMT slanders us as "bandits." Since "the CCP are bandits and Chang the third is a communist, Chang the third is a bandit." We say: "Since the KMT are bandits and Chiang

[27] Yuan Shih-k'ai (1859–1916) rose to power from 1896 onwards. From 1901 to 1908 he had been the strong man of China, holding the post of the viceroy of the metropolitan province. His recall in 1911 led to a compromise with the revolutionaries and his succession to Sun Yat-sen as the President of China. In 1915–6 he attempted to found a dynasty of his own, a venture which ended in failure and his early death.

[28] These prefaces, or more often postscripts, are not intended for publication; they are more like students' essays, written to clarify the writers' minds after reading a book.

Kai-shek is a member of the KMT, Chiang is a bandit." Both these statements conform to formal logic.

Not much new knowledge can be acquired by using formal logic. Of course there is deduction [in it], but in fact the conclusion [arrived at by using formal logic] is already contained in the major premises. Some people confuse formal logic with dialectics. This is wrong.

# 5

# Poetry

## INSCRIPTION ON A PHOTOGRAPH OF THE CAVE OF THE IMMORTALS, LUSHAN, TAKEN BY COMRADE LI CHIN,[1] *CH'I-CHÜEH* (September 9, 1961)[2]

The sinewy pine is seen in the dimness of twilight,
Unperturbed by the fleecy clouds that hurry by.
The Cave of the Immortals is a work of nature.
Much charm resides in these craggy peaks.

## CHINGKANGSHAN REVISITED (TO THE MELODY OF *SHUI TIAO KO T'OU*) (1965)[3]

A long cherished wish to approach the clouds
Once more, by climbing the Chingkang Mountains.
After a journey of a thousand leagues
The old view seen in a new visage.
Everywhere orioles sing, swallows dart,
Brooks murmur,

[1] According to Peking *Chingkangshan*, a Red Guard newspaper under the influence of Chiang Ch'ing (Mme. Mao), the picture was taken by Chiang Ch'ing herself. It is certain that when she was adopted by her maternal grandfather, Chiang changed her family name from Luan to Li, but it is never sure whether her given name was Yün-ho or Ch'ing-yün. Chin might well be her given name. She adopted the stage name of Lan P'ing in 1934 and the present name, Chiang Ch'ing, in 1940. The issue of Peking *Chingkangshan* in which Chiang Ch'ing is eulogized was published on May 25, 1967, and translated into English by the American Consulate in Hong Kong, in *Survey of China Mainland Press*, No. 3996, August 8, 1967.

[2] Translated by Michael Bullock and Jerome Ch'en, in *Mao and the Chinese Revolution* (London, New York, 1965), p. 354. Reprinted by permission of Oxford University Press.

[3] From the *China Quarterly*, No. 34 (April–June, 1968). Reprinted by permission of *China Quarterly*. For notes and explanations to this poem, see Professor Takeuchi Minoru's discussion below, pp. 142–45.

And the tall tree[4] brushes clouds.
Once past Huangyangchieh
Do not look down the precipices.

Wind and thunder rumbled;
Banners unfurled;
The realm was made stable.
Thirty-eight years have elapsed
Like a snap of the fingers.
Reach the ninth heaven high to embrace the moon
 Or the five oceans deep to capture a turtle: either is possible.
Return to merriment and triumphant songs.
Under this heaven nothing is difficult,
If only there is the will to ascend.

[4] Under this tree, Mao and Chu Teh used to sit and discuss tactics.

# 6

## Imperialism and American Imperialism

### NUCLEAR WEAPONS ARE PAPER TIGERS (August, 1946)[1]

The atom bomb is a paper tiger which the U.S. reactionaries use to scare people. It looks terrible, but in fact it isn't. Of course, the atom bomb is a weapon of mass slaughter, but the outcome of a war is decided by the people, not by one or two new types of weapon.

All reactionaries are paper tigers. In appearance, the reactionaries are terrifying, but in reality they are not so powerful. From a long-term point of view, it is not the reactionaries but the people who are really powerful. In Russia, before the February Revolution in 1917, which side was really strong? On the surface the tsar was strong but he was swept away by a single gust of wind in the February Revolution. In the final analysis, the strength in Russia was on the side of the Soviets of Workers, Peasants and Soldiers. The tsar was just a paper tiger. Wasn't Hitler once considered very strong? But history proved that he was a paper tiger. So was Mussolini, so was Japanese imperialism. On the contrary, the strength of the Soviet Union and of the people in all countries who loved democracy and freedom proved much greater than had been foreseen.

Chiang Kai-shek and his supporters, the U.S. reactionaries, are all paper tigers too. Speaking of the U.S. imperialism, people seem to feel that it is terrifically strong. Chinese reactionaries are using the "strength" of the United States to frighten the Chinese people. But it will be proved that the U.S. reactionaries, like all the reac-

[1] From "Talk with the American Correspondent Anna Louise Strong," *HC*, IV, 1192–93, or *SW*, IV, 100–101.

tionaries in history, do not have much strength. In the United States there are others who are really strong—the American people.

Take the case of China. We have only millet plus rifles to rely on, but history will finally prove that our millet plus rifles is more powerful than Chiang Kai-shek's aeroplanes plus tanks. Although the Chinese people still face many difficulties and will long suffer hardships from the joint attacks of U.S. imperialism and the Chinese reactionaries, the day will come when these reactionaries are defeated and we are victorious. The reason is simply this: the reactionaries represent reaction, we represent progress.

### A SPEECH DELIVERED AT THE EIGHTH MEETING OF THE GOVERNMENT COUNCIL OF THE PEOPLE'S REPUBLIC OF CHINA (June 28, 1950)[2]

The Chinese people have long since affirmed that the affairs of the various countries throughout the world should be run by the peoples of these countries, and that the affairs of Asia should be run by the peoples of Asia and not by the United States. U.S. aggression in Asia will only arouse widespread and resolute resistance by the peoples of Asia. Truman stated on January 5 this year that the United States would not interfere in Taiwan. Now he has proved his own statement to be false, and has torn to shreds all the international agreements regarding non-interference by the United States in the internal affairs of China. The United States has thus exposed its own imperialist face and this is beneficial to the people of China and of all of Asia. There is no reason at all for U.S. intervention in the internal affairs of Korea, the Philippines, Vietnam or other countries. The sympathy of the people throughout China, as well as of the broad masses of the people everywhere in the world, is on the side of the victims of aggression and most decidedly not on the side of U.S. imperialism. The people will neither be bought by imperialism nor cowed by it. Imperialism is outwardly strong but feeble within, because it has no support among the people. People throughout China and the world! Unite and prepare fully to defeat any provocation by U.S. imperialism.

[2] From *Shih-chieh chih-shih*, No. 20 (October 20, 1958).

**A SPEECH AT THE SUPREME STATE CONFERENCE (September 8, 1958)[3]**

U.S. imperialism invaded China's territory of Taiwan and has occupied it for the past nine years. A short while ago it sent its armed forces to invade and occupy the Lebanon. The United States has set up hundreds of military bases in many countries all over the world. The Chinese territory Taiwan, the Lebanon, and all U.S. military bases on foreign territories are like nooses tied round the necks of the U.S. imperialists. The Americans themselves, and nobody else, made these nooses, and they themselves put them round their own necks and handed the ends of the ropes to the Chinese people, the peoples of the Arab countries and all the peoples of the world who love peace and oppose aggression. The longer the U.S. aggressors remain in these places, the tighter the nooses round their necks will become.

The U.S. imperialists have been creating tension in all parts of the world in attempts to achieve their aggressive ends and to enslave the peoples of various countries. The U.S. imperialists calculate that they will always benefit from tense situations, but the fact is that the tense situations created by the United States have led to the opposite of what the Americans wish. They serve, in effect, to mobilize the people of the world to oppose the U.S. aggressors.

If the U.S. monopoly capitalist group is bent on carrying out its policy of aggression and war, the day will certainly come when humanity will hang it by the neck. A similar fate awaits the accomplices of the United States.

**CALLING UPON THE PEOPLE OF THE WORLD TO UNITE TO OPPOSE RACIAL DISCRIMINATION BY U.S. IMPERIALISM AND SUPPORT THE AMERICAN NEGROES IN THEIR STRUGGLE AGAINST RACIAL DISCRIMINATION (August 8, 1963)[4]**

The speedy development of the struggle of the American Negroes is a manifestation of the sharpening of class struggle and na-

---

[3] From *Peking Review*, No. 37 (November 11, 1958).
[4] From *Peking Review*, April 16, 1963, pp. 6–7.

tional struggle within the United States; it has been causing increasing anxiety to the U.S. ruling circles. The Kennedy Administration has resorted to cunning two-faced tactics. On the one hand, it continues to connive at and take part in the discrimination against and persecution of Negroes; it even sends troops to suppress them. On the other hand, it is parading as an advocate of "the defence of human rights" and "the protection of the rights of Negroes," is calling upon the Negro people to exercise "restraint," is proposing to Congress the so-called "civil rights legislation," in an attempt to lull the fighting will of the Negro people and deceive the masses throughout the country. However, these tactics of the Kennedy Administration are being seen through by more and more of the Negroes. The fascist atrocities committed by the U.S. imperialists against the Negro people have laid bare the true nature of the so-called democracy and freedom in the United States and revealed the inner link between the reactionary policies pursued by the U.S. Government at home and its policies of agression abroad.

I call upon the workers, peasants, revolutionary intellectuals, enlightened elements of the bourgeoisie and other enlightened personages of all colours in the world, white, black, yellow, brown, etc., to unite to oppose the racial discrimination practised by U.S. imperialism and to support the American Negroes in their struggle against racial discrimination. In the final analysis, a national struggle is a question of class struggle. In the United States, it is only the reactionary ruling circles among the whites who are oppressing the Negro people. They can in no way represent the enlightened persons who comprise the overwhelming majority of the white people. At present, it is the handful of imperialists, headed by the United States, and their supporters, the reactionaries in different countries, who are carrying out oppression, aggression and intimidation against the overwhelming majority of the nations and peoples of the world. We are in the majority and they are in the minority. At most, they make up less than 10 percent of the 3,000 million population of the world. I am firmly convinced that, with the support of more than 90 percent of the people of the world, the American Negroes will be victorious in their just struggle. The evil system of colonialism and imperialism grew up along with the enslavement of Negroes and the trade in Negroes, it will surely come to its end with the thorough emancipation of the black people.

## ON THE AFRO-AMERICANS' STRUGGLES (1968) [5]

The Afro-American struggle is not only a struggle waged by the exploited and oppressed black people for freedom and emancipation, it is also a new clarion call to all the exploited and oppressed people of the United States to fight against the barbarous rule of the monopoly capitalist class. It is a tremendous aid and inspiration to the struggle of the people throughout the world against United States imperialism and to the struggle of the Vietnamese people against United States imperialism. On behalf of the Chinese people, I hereby express resolute support for the just struggle of the black people in the United States.

Racial discrimination in the United States is a product of the colonialist and imperialist system. The contradiction between the black masses in the United States and United States ruling circles is a class contradiction. Only by overthrowing the reactionary rule of the United States monopoly capitalist class and destroying the colonialist and imperialist system can the black people in the United States win complete emancipation. The black masses and the masses of white working people in the United States have common interests and common objectives to struggle for. Therefore, the Afro-American struggle is winning sympathy and support from increasing numbers of white working people and progressives in the United States. The struggle of the black people in the United States is bound to merge with the American workers' movement and eventually end the criminal rule of the United States monopoly capitalist class.

In 1963, in the "Statement Supporting the Afro-Americans in Their Just Struggle against Racial Discrimination by United States Imperialism," I said that "the evil system of colonialism and imperialism grew up along with the enslavement of Negroes and the trade in Negroes, and it will surely come to its end with the thorough emancipation of the black people." I still maintain this view.

[5] From a statement made after the assassination of Dr. Martin Luther King on April 16, 1968. *NCNA* (*New China News Agency*), April 16, 1968. *Summary of World Broadcasts*, FE/2747/A1/1, April 18, 1968. Reprinted by permission of The British Broadcasting Corporation.

# 7
# The Soviet Union

After the death of Lenin, Comrade Stalin guided the people of the Soviet Union and made the first socialist country in the world he and the illustrious Lenin had created during the October Revolution into a brilliant socialist society. The victory of the socialist construction is not a victory of the people of the Soviet Union alone; it is also a victory of all the peoples of the world. . . .

Since the death of Lenin, Comrade Stalin had always been the central figure of the world communist movement. We surrounded him, ceaselessly asked guidance from him, and continuously drew ideological strength from his writings. Comrade Stalin had unbounded affection for the oppressed peoples of the East. "Don't forget the East!" was his clarion call after the October Revolution. Everyone knows that Comrade Stalin passionately loved the Chinese people and regarded their revolutionary potentials as limitless. On the question of the Chinese revolution, he devoted his noble wisdom. The Chinese communist party and Chinese people, having followed the theories of Lenin and Stalin and had the support of the revolutionary forces of the great Soviet republics and other countries, won their historic victory a few years ago.

Now, we have lost our great teacher and most sincere friend— Comrade Stalin. This is a sad blow! The sorrow it has brought to us is beyond description.

Our task is to transform the sorrow into strength. For commemorating our great teacher, Stalin, the Chinese communist party and Chinese people will together with the Soviet communist party and people, in the name of Stalin, unlimitedly consolidate our great friendship. The Chinese communist party and the Chinese people will intensify their study of Stalin's theories and learn the science

[1] From *Tsui-wei-ta ti yu-i* [The greatest friendship] (Peking, 1953), pp. 2–6.

and technology of the Soviet Union, for the construction of our country. . . .

The great friendship between the Chinese and Soviet peoples is indestructible, because it is based on the internationalist principles of Marx, Engels, Lenin, and Stalin. The friendship between the Chinese and the Soviet peoples on the one hand and the peoples of the people's democracies and all those who love peace, democracy, and justice on the other is founded on the same principles, and therefore is indestructible too.

It is obvious that the strength derived from this kind of friendship is inexhaustible and invincible.

## MAO, PARTY, AND THE SOVIET UNION

### Conversation with the Japanese Socialist Delegation
### Led by Sasaki Kozo, Peking, July 10, 1964 [2]

The areas occupied by the Soviet Union are really too many. By the Yalta Agreement, under the guise of making her independent, Mongolia actually came under the control of the Soviet Union. Mongolia is far greater than Chishima (Kuriles). In 1954 when Khrushchev and Bulganin came to China, we raised this question [the territorial question], but they turned us down. They [the Soviet Union] took a part of Rumania for their own; they also partitioned off East Germany and drove its people to the West. They partitioned a part of Poland and annexed it to Russia, and in compensation transferred a part of East Germany to Poland. The same sort of thing happened with Finland. Wherever they can detach, they have done so to the limit. It is said that Sinkiang and north of the Amur River must be incorporated into the Soviet Union. The Soviet Union is massing troops toward the frontiers.

The Soviet Union has an area of 22,000,000 square kilometers and a population of only 200 million. It should stop [its] activities of annexation. Japan has 370,000 square kilometers and a population of 100 million. About 100 years ago the areas east of Baikal came under Russian occupation, and since then Vladivostok, Kha-

---

[2] From *The Sekai Shuho* [The World Weekly] (Tokyo), August 11, 1964, p. 37. Translated by Trevor Leggett. Reprinted by permission of *The Sekai Shuho*.

barovsk, Kamchatka, and so on became Soviet territory. We have not yet had the reckoning for this account. From our point of view there can be no question about Chishima—they should be returned to Japan.

### Interview with André Malraux (Peking, 1965) [3]

Mao reflects. "Plekhanov and the Mensheviks were Marxists, even Leninists. They cut themselves off from the masses and ended up by taking up arms against the Bolsheviks—or rather they mainly ended up exiled or shot.

"There are now two paths for every communist: that of socialist construction, and that of revisionism. We are beyond the bark-eating stage, but we have only got as far as a bowl of rice a day. To accept revisionism is to snatch away the bowl of rice. As I told you, we made the Revolution with peasant rebels; then we led them against the cities ruled by the Kuomintang. But the successor of the Kuomintang was not the Chinese Communist party, however important that may be: it was the *New Democracy*. The history of the Revolution, like the weakness of the proletariat of the big cities, forced the communists into collaboration with the petty bourgeoisie. For that reason, too, our revolution, in the last analysis, will no more resemble the Russian Revolution than the Russian Revolution resembled yours. Even today, broad layers of our society are conditioned in such a way that their activity is necessarily orientated toward revisionism. They can only obtain what they want by taking it from the masses."

(I think of Stalin: "We did not bring about the October Revolution in order to give power to the kulaks!")

"Corruption, law-breaking, the arrogance of intellectuals, the wish to do honor to one's family by becoming a white-collar worker and not dirtying one's hands anymore, all these stupidities are only symptoms. Inside the party and out. The cause of them is the historical conditions themselves. But also the political conditions."

[3] From André Malraux, *Anti-Memoirs*, trans. Terence Kilmartin (London, New York, 1968), pp. 369–70, 373–74. Copyright © 1968 by Holt, Rinehart & Winston, Inc., and Hamish Hamilton Ltd. Reprinted by permission of Holt, Rinehart & Winston, Inc., and Hamish Hamilton Ltd.

I know his theory: you begin by no longer tolerating criticism, then you abandon self-criticism, then you cut yourself off from the masses, and, since the party can draw its revolutionary strength only from them, you tolerate the formation of a new class; finally like Khrushchev, you proclaim peaceful coexistence on a durable basis with the United States—and the Americans arrive in Vietnam. I have not forgotten his old saying: "Here seventy percent of the people are poor peasants, and their sense of the Revolution has never been at fault." He has just explained how he interprets it: one must learn from the masses in order to be able to teach them.

"That is why," he says, "Soviet revisionism is an . . . apostasy."

＊　　＊　　＊

". . . When he [Khrushchev] came here for the last time, on his return from Camp David, he believed in compromise with American imperialism. He imagined that the Soviet government was that of all Russia. He imagined that the contradictions had almost disappeared there. The truth is that if the contradictions due to victory are less painful than the old ones, luckily they are almost as deep. Humanity left to its own devices does not necessarily reestablish capitalism (which is why you are perhaps right in saying they will not revert to private ownership of the means of production), but it does reestablish inequality. The forces tending toward the creation of new classes are powerful. We have just suppressed military titles and badges of rank; every 'cadre' becomes a worker again at least one day a week; whole trainloads of city dwellers go off to work in the people's communes. Khrushchev seemed to think that a revolution is done when a communist party has seized power —as if it were merely a question of national liberation. . . .

"Lenin was well aware that at this juncture the revolution is only just beginning. The forces and traditions he was referring to are not only the legacy of the bourgeoisie. They are also our fate. . . . The revisionists mix up cause and effect. Equality is not important in itself; it is important because it is natural to those who have not lost contact with the masses. . . . You remember Kosygin at the Twenty-third Congress: 'Communism means the raising of living standards.' Of course! And swimming is a way of putting on a pair of trunks! Stalin had destroyed the kulaks. It isn't simply a question of replacing the Tsar with Khrushchev, one bourgeoisie with another, even if it's called communist. . . . The thought, culture, and customs which brought China to where we found her must disappear, the thought, customs, and culture of proletarian China, which does not yet exist, must appear."

# PART TWO

# MAO VIEWED BY HIS CONTEMPORARIES

*The quoted items in this small collection are from scholars or journalists who have authoritative knowledge of Mao or from people in authoritative positions. Therefore, either the words themselves carry weight or they derive their importance from the authority of their authors. Except for the man and his cult, this collection is meant to be an extension of Part One, incorporating views on Mao's military and political lines with respect to China's internal and external developments.*

# 8

# The Man and the Cult

## EDGAR SNOW ON MAO (1936)[1]

*Edgar Snow, well-known American journalist who has visited China many times both before and after the 1949 revolution, gained international recognition with his report on the Chinese Communist movement in 1937.* Red Star over China, *which contains Mao's autobiography as told to the author, is a pioneer work, published at a time when the world knew almost nothing about the movement led by Mao; because of its reliability this work has established itself as an indispensable source of information. It has been translated into all*

---

[1] From Edgar Snow, *Red Star over China* (London, 1937), pp. 79–80, 81–82, 83, 84, 87, 88. Copyright © 1938, 1944 by Random House, Inc. Copyright © 1968 by Edgar Snow. Reprinted by permission of Grove Press, Inc., Linden and Deutsch, Victor Gollancz Ltd., and the author.

*the major languages of the world, including Chinese. Snow is*
*also the author of* Random Notes on Red China *(Cambridge,*
*Mass., 1957) and* The Other Side of the River *(New York, 1962).*

I met Mao soon after my arrival: a gaunt, rather Lincolnesque
figure, above average height for a Chinese, somewhat stooped, with
a head of thick black hair grown very long, and with large, searching eyes, a high-bridged nose and prominent cheek-bones.

\* \* \*

I happened to be in his house one evening when he was given a
complete physical examination by a Red surgeon—a returned student from Europe who knew his business—and pronounced in excellent health. He has never had tuberculosis or any "incurable
disease," as has been rumoured by some romantic travellers. His
lungs are completely sound, although, unlike most Red commanders, he is an inordinate cigarette-smoker. During the Long March,
Mao and Li Teh (another heavy smoker) carried on original bo-
tanical research by testing out various kinds of leaves as tobacco
substitutes.

\* \* \*

Mao seemed to me a very interesting and complex man. He had
the simplicity and naturalness of the Chinese peasant, with a lively
sense of humour and love of rustic laughter. His laughter was even
active on the subject of himself and the shortcomings of the Soviets
—a boyish sort of laughter which never in the least shook his inner
faith in his purpose. He is plain-speaking and plain-living, and
some people might think him rather coarse and vulgar. Yet he
combines curious qualities of naïveté with the most incisive wit
and worldly sophistication.

I think my first impression—dominantly one of native shrewdness
—was probably correct. And yet Mao is an accomplished scholar of
Classical Chinese, an omnivorous reader, a deep student of philosophy and history, a good speaker, a man with an unusual memory
and extraordinary powers of concentration, an able writer, careless

in his personal habits and appearance but astonishingly meticulous about details of duty, a man of tireless energy, and a military and political strategist of considerable genius. It is an interesting fact that many Japanese regard him as the ablest Chinese strategist alive.

*  *  *

He appeared to be quite free from symptoms of megalomania, but he has a deep sense of personal dignity, and something about him suggests a power of ruthless decision when he deems it necessary. I never saw him angry, but I heard from others that on occasions he has been roused to an intense and withering fury. At such times his command of irony and invective is said to be classic and lethal.

*  *  *

Mao impressed me as a man of considerable depth of feeling. I remember that his eyes moistened once or twice when speaking of dead comrades, or recalling incidents in his youth, during the rice riots and famines of Hunan, when some starving peasants were beheaded in his province for demanding food from the yamen. One soldier told me of seeing Mao give his coat away to a wounded man at the front. They say that he refused to wear shoes when the Red warriors had none.

*  *  *

He seemed to me sincere, honest, and truthful in his statements. I was able to check up on many of his assertions, and usually found them to be correct. He subjected me to mild doses of political propaganda, but nothing compared with what I have received in non-bandit quarters, and he never imposed any censorship on me, either in my writing or photography, courtesies for which I was grateful. He did his best to see that I got facts to explain various aspects of Soviet life.

### EDGAR SNOW ON MAO (1960)[2]

On the day I first visited Mao in the Imperial City I saw only two sentries at the New Gate by which we entered. Just west of it stands the great T'ien An Men, on the wide busy main thoroughfare called Ch'ang An Chieh (Long Peace Way). Across from it is the marble-columned Great Hall of the People. Mao frequently walks from his home to the Great Hall followed by a few plain-clothes men. Within the compound no guards were visible along a willow-fringed drive that skirted the palace lakes, past beds of gladioli and chrysanthemums, to the graceful old one-story yellow-roofed residence. It is one of a group of palace buildings formerly occupied by court mandarins and later by Kuomintang officials. Most members of the Politburo are similarly quartered, close to each other. The great chambers and audience halls of the main palaces are now museums or playgrounds and in one corner of Pei Hai stands a model nursery.

Mao's family consists of his wife, his daughter, and a grown son. The son is an engineer and now works obscurely in the provinces. Mao's daughter, by his present wife, is a student at Peking University. Mme Mao (Lan P'ing), a comely moving-picture actress from Shanghai when she married Mao in 1939 in Yenan, has long been in poor health and is rarely seen in public. She and the children are seldom mentioned in the press.

The large, comfortable living room of Mao's home is tastefully furnished in Chinese style; directly adjoining it are [a] small dining room and his study and living quarters. The meals he eats and serves his guests are a few home-style dishes of Hunanese cooking. He drank with me a bit of *mao-t'ai,* a fiery liquor of Hunan, in raising toasts for the occasion. He also served the Chinese red table wine which was for sale (unrationed) in the liquor stores of North China at one yuan a bottle.

Mao is much heavier than he used to be; he eats moderately and smokes fewer cigarettes. For a man close to seventy, oftentimes re-

[2] Condensed from Edgar Snow, *The Other Side of the River* (New York, 1962), pp. 151–56. Copyright © 1962 by Edgar Snow. Reprinted by permission of Random House, Inc., Linden and Deutsch, Victor Gollancz Ltd., and the author.

ported dead, he was "holding the status quo," as he put it, and had had no serious illness for many years. He wore a plain dark gray woolen jacket buttoned at the neck, with trousers to match; this has been a kind of official uniform ever since Sun Yat-sen introduced it. Mao had on brown leather shoes in need of a polish, and cotton socks hung loosely at his ankles. . . .

Many of Mao's disappearances from public view are long periods of solitary study. He may spend as much as a whole week reading, a habit acquired in his youth. He once left a middle school he was attending because "its regulations were objectionable," and spent the term "reading every day in the Hunan Provincial Library."

### ANDRÉ MALRAUX ON MAO (1965)[3]

*Prominent novelist and man of action, Malraux made his first association with China in the 1920's, and his book,* The Human Condition, *brilliantly portrayed the ethos of that old country in convulsion. When he interviewed Mao in 1965, he was Minister of Culture of General de Gaulle's Government.*

The man walking slowly by my side is haunted by something more than the uninterrupted revolution; by a gigantic conception of which neither of us has spoken: the underdeveloped countries are far more numerous than the countries of the West, and the struggle began as soon as the colonies became nations. He knows that he will not see the global revolution. The underdeveloped nations are at the same stage as the proletariat in 1848. But there will be a Marx (he himself first and foremost) and a Lenin. A great deal can be done in a century! It is not a question of the alliance of such and such an external proletariat with an internal proletariat, the alliance of India with the British Labour movement, of Algeria with the French communists; it is a question of the vast tracts of misery against the little European headland, against hateful America. Proletariat will unite with capitalism, as in Russia, as

[3] From André Malraux, *Anti-Memoirs,* trans. Terence Kilmartin (London, New York, 1968), pp. 376–77. Copyright © 1968 by Holt, Rinehart & Winston, Inc., and Hamish Hamilton Ltd. Reprinted by permission of Holt, Rinehart & Winston, Inc., and Hamish Hamilton Ltd.

in the United States. But there is one country dedicated to vengeance and justice, one country that will never lay down its arms, will never lay down its spirit, before the global confrontation. Three hundred years of European energy are now on the wane; the Chinese era is dawning. He reminded me of the emperors, and he now reminds me, standing there, of the rust-covered shields of the army chiefs which belonged to the funerary avenues of the emperors, and are to be found abandoned in the sorghum fields. Behind our entire conversation the hope of a twilight world stood watch. In the vast corridor, the dignitaries have stopped, without daring to turn round. . . .

The car drives off. I draw back the little curtains on the rear window. As when I arrived, but this time in broad daylight, he is alone in his dark costume at the center of a slightly withdrawn circle of light-colored suits. . . . Overhead, an airplane flashes past. With his hand to his forehead in the age-old gesture, the Old Man of the Mountain watches it recede, shading his eyes from the sun.

## CHANG JU-HSIN ON THE GREATNESS OF MAO (1946)[4]

*Chang Ju-hsin was one of the first champions of the cult of Mao. A teacher at a party school, he published "Study and grasp of Mao Tse-tung's theory and tactics," in the* Liberation Daily *(Yenan), February 18 and 19, 1942. Later, in a party periodical, the* Northern Culture *(Nos. 1–4), he published articles on Mao's view of life, scientific methods, scientific prophesy, and style, which were reprinted in pamphlet form by the Northeast Bookshop and in Hong Kong in 1946. Since 1949, he seems to have fallen out of Mao's favor and into oblivion.*

The greatness of Mao Tse-tung lies in his deep understanding of the feelings and wishes of the masses, his familiarity with their experiences and creativeness, and his guidance in serving them with the programs, policies, and methods which he has systematically formulated on the basis of his investigations, studies, analyses,

[4] From *Mao Tse-tung Lun* [On Mao Tse-tung], a series of lectures delivered at the North China Associated University, 1946, pp. 12–13.

and syntheses in every period of the past. All his ideas, statements, policies, and methods have come from the broad masses and gone back to them. Some people say that Mao Tse-tung is a genius, a wise man. Certainly, he is the greatest genius since the beginning of the history of China. But it must be pointed out that his genius is neither a mystery nor the result of some inborn qualities. His genius, wisdom, and intelligence are the concentrated reflection of those of the Chinese people. Mao Tse-tung is the most outstanding descendant of the Yellow Emperor,[5] the most distinguished representative of the Chinese people. At the same time, he is also a leader of the people of the world, a scientist, a genius, and a revolutionary—a faithful disciple of Marx, Engels, Lenin, and Stalin. He has combined Marxist theory which is the crystallization of the scientific thoughts of several thousand years and the rich and vigorous practice of the Chinese revolution. He serves the broad masses by applying the scientific methods of Marxism and by starting from the reality of China, and thus satisfies the feelings and wishes of the broad masses. Consequently, he has been able, in the protracted revolutionary struggle of China, to concentrate their genius, wisdom, and intelligence and to transform them into his own genius, wisdom, and intelligence so as to guide the emancipation of the Chinese people.

### EDGAR SNOW ON THE WORSHIP OF MAO [6]

The cult built around Mao is also no new phenomenon. Chiang [Kai-shek] made a fair start toward self-deification; before him there was the Sun Yat-sen cult, and before Sun there were the emperors and emperor worship. Nations which for centuries have been ruled by authoritarianism may cast aside one skin and pick up another but they do not change chromosomes, genes and bodies in a generation or two.

*       *       *

[5] A legendary figure believed to be the primogenitor of the Han-Chinese. The legend was revived during the 1900's as an attempt to restore the self-confidence of the Han-Chinese.

[6] Condensed from Edgar Snow, *The Other Side of the River* (New York, 1962), pp. 122, 150–51. Copyright © 1962 by Edgar Snow. Reprinted by permission of Random House, Inc., Linden and Deutsch, Victor Gollancz Ltd., and the author.

Today's image of Mao among the masses is hardly that of an executioner. What makes him formidable is that he is not just a party boss but by many millions of Chinese is quite genuinely regarded as a teacher, statesman, strategist, philosopher, poet laureate, national hero, head of the family, and greatest liberator in history. He is to them Confucius plus Lao-tzu plus Rousseau plus Marx plus Buddha. . . .

Some of the hero worship of Mao may express much of the same kind of national self-esteem as British idolatry of Queen Victoria in days when the Empire was shouldering the white man's burden. Victoria did no more to discourage that, it may be recalled, than the press is doing to demolish the Kennedy "image" of today. In so far as the Mao "cult" is reminiscent of the synthetic beatification of Stalin when he was alive, it is to any Westerner nauseating in the same degree. No public building, no commune, no factory or girls' dormitory is complete without its solemn statue or plaster bust of the man with the mole on his chin. They are as much a part of the furniture in any reception room as the inevitable green table cloth and bowls of boiling tea. . . .

The value of a state father image in the "democratic dictatorship" is clearly recognized by the Chinese party. With the breakup of large families as a result of industrialization of both town and country, as well as the replacement of family paternalism by party paternalism, the mantle of national patriarch would inevitably have descended on the shoulders of any leader in a country not far removed from ancestor worship and emperor worship. Mao has now become an Institution of such prestige and authority that no one in the party could raze it without sacrificing a collective vested interest of first importance. Probably no one knows that better than Mao himself.

**THE DEPUTY CHIEF EDITOR OF THE MOLODAYA GVARDIYA PUBLISHING HOUSE ON THE WORSHIP OF MAO, MOSCOW RADIO (January 21, 1967)[7]**

*The author was in China with a group of young Russian tourists in the first, also the most violent, phase of the Cultural Revolution.*

[7] From *Survey* (London), April, 1967, pp. 192–93. Reprinted by permission of *Survey*.

The so-called Great Proletarian Cultural Revolution in China is also a sad demonstration of the extent to which the public deification of Mao Tse-tung has now been carried. The Red Guards consider that Mao is their commander-in-chief and that they are his soldiers. The notion that it is not Marxism-Leninism which is now the ideology of the Chinese Communist Party, but the ideas of Mao Tse-tung, is being instilled in the younger generation with all the weapons in the ideological armoury. Recently the Minister of Defence, Lin Piao, declared unashamedly: "Chairman Mao is much greater than Marx, Engels, Lenin, and Stalin; there is at present no other man in the world who could be placed next to Chairman Mao." It is asserted in China that 99 percent of the time the Chinese spend studying the classics of Marxism must be devoted to the study of Mao's works [instead], because they alone can form the text-book of revolution.

Mao Tse-tung also appears to the people like a god. He does not talk to the Red Guards, he only poses in front of them and the cine-cameras. During a period of one and a half months Mao Tse-tung made about 10 appearances at meetings on Tienanmen Square, but at none of them did he utter a single word. The spot on the Square where he sat on October 1 to watch the fireworks display after descending from the rostrum of Heavenly Peace (Tien-an) is now considered to be in the nature of a sacred spot. The papers keep on writing about it; they describe how masses of Red Guards stream to the spot, full of joy that they can see the place where Chairman Mao sat. We watched them swear their oath of loyalty there, and saw how they rubbed off the red paint from the brick wall to put a finger-mark in their little red books in commemoration of this memorable occasion.

# 9
## Lin Piao, "Long Live the Victory of People's War!"[1]

*Marshal Lin Piao (1907– ) is now widely believed to be Mao's successor. Trained at Chiang Kai-shek's Whampoa Military Academy near Canton, he took part in the Northern Expedition before the split of the Kuomintang-Communist alliance in 1927. In less than two years, from 1927–1929, he had risen from a major in the Red Army to a general. A brilliant strategist, he distinguished himself in the Long March, the Resistance War against Japan, and the civil war in which he was the commander of the largest field army, which swept across China and brought the Communist revolution to victory. After initial successes in Korea as the commanding officer of the Chinese army, he retired from active service, probably due to ill health, but was elected to the Politburo. In 1959, he replaced P'eng Teh-huai as the Minister of Defense and initiated a drastic reorganization of the People's Liberation Army of China.*

Comrade Mao Tse-tung's theory of people's war has been proved by the long practice of the Chinese revolution to be in accord with the objective laws of such wars and to be invincible. It has not only been valid for China, it is a great contribution to the revolutionary struggles of the oppressed nations and peoples throughout the world.

The people's war led by the Chinese Communist Party, comprising the War of Resistance and the Revolutionary Civil Wars, lasted for twenty-two years. It constitutes the most drawn-out and

[1] From *Peking Review*, September 3, 1965, pp. 9–30.

most complex people's war led by the proletariat in modern history, and it has been the richest in experience.

In the last analysis, the Marxist-Leninist theory of proletarian revolution is the theory of the seizure of state power by revolutionary violence, the theory of countering war against the people by people's war. As Marx so aptly put it, "Force is the midwife of every old society pregnant with a new one."

It was on the basis of the lessons derived from the people's wars in China that Comrade Mao Tse-tung, using the simplest and the most vivid language, advanced the famous thesis that "political power grows out of the barrel of a gun."

He clearly pointed out:

> The seizure of power by armed force, the settlement of the issue by war, is the central task and the highest form of revolution. This Marxist-Leninist principle of revolution holds good universally, for China and for all other countries.

War is the product of imperialism and the system of exploitation of man by man. Lenin said that "war is always and everywhere begun by the exploiters themselves, by the ruling and oppressing classes." So long as imperialism and the system of exploitation of man by man exist, the imperialists and reactionaries will invariably rely on armed force to maintain their reactionary rule and impose war on the oppressed nations and peoples. This is an objective law independent of man's will.

In the world today, all the imperialists headed by the United States and their lackeys, without exception, are strengthening their state machinery, and especially their armed forces. U.S. imperialism, in particular, is carrying out armed aggression and suppression everywhere.

What should the oppressed nations and the oppressed people do in the face of wars of aggression and armed suppression by the imperialists and their lackeys? Should they submit and remain slaves in perpetuity? Or should they rise in resistance and fight for their liberation?

Comrade Mao Tse-tung answered this question in vivid terms. He said that after long investigation and study the Chinese people discovered that all the imperialists and their lackeys "have swords in their hands and are out to kill. The people have come to understand this and so act after the same fashion." This is called doing unto them what they do unto us.

In the last analysis, whether one dares to wage a tit-for-tat struggle against armed aggression and suppression by the imperialists and their lackeys, whether one dares to fight a people's war against them, is tantamount to whether one dares to embark on revolution. This is the most effective touchstone for distinguishing genuine from fake revolutionaries and Marxist-Leninists.

In view of the fact that some people were afflicted with the fear of the imperialists and reactionaries, Comrade Mao Tse-tung put forward his famous thesis that the "imperialists and all reactionaries are paper tigers." He said:

> All reactionaries are paper tigers. In appearance, the reactionaries are terrifying, but in reality they are not so powerful. From a long-term point of view, it is not the reactionaries but the people who are really powerful.

The history of people's war in China and other countries provides conclusive evidence that the growth of the people's revolutionary forces from weak and small beginnings into strong and large forces is a universal law of development of class struggle, a universal law of development of people's war. A people's war inevitably meets with many difficulties, with ups and downs and setbacks in the course of its development, but no force can alter its general trend toward inevitable triumph.

Comrade Mao Tse-tung points out that we must despise the enemy strategically and take full account of him tactically.

To despise the enemy strategically is an elementary requirement for a revolutionary. Without the courage to despise the enemy and without daring to win, it will be simply impossible to make revolution and wage a people's war, let alone to achieve victory.

It is also very important for revolutionaries to take full account of the enemy tactically. It is likewise impossible to win victory in a people's war without taking full account of the enemy tactically, and without examining the concrete conditions, without being prudent and giving great attention to the study of the art of struggle, and without adopting appropriate forms of struggle in the concrete practice of the revolution in each country and with regard to each concrete problem of struggle.

Dialectical and historical materialism teaches us that what is important primarily is not that which at the given moment seems to be durable and yet is already beginning to die away, but that which is arising and developing, even though at the given moment it may not appear to be durable, for only that which is arising and developing is invincible.

Why can the apparently weak new-born forces always triumph over the decadent forces which appear so powerful? The reason is that truth is on their side and that the masses are on their side, while the reactionary classes are always divorced from the masses and set themselves against the masses.

This has been borne out by the victory of the Chinese revolution, by the history of all revolutions, the whole history of class struggle and the entire history of mankind.

The imperialists are extremely afraid of Comrade Mao Tse-tung's thesis that "imperialism and all reactionaries are paper tigers," and the revisionists are extremely hostile to it. They all oppose and attack this thesis and the philistines follow suit by ridiculing it. But all this cannot in the least diminish its importance. The light of truth cannot be dimmed by anybody.

Comrade Mao Tse-tung's theory of people's war solves not only the problem of daring to fight a people's war, but also that of how to wage it.

Comrade Mao Tse-tung is a great statesman and military scientist, proficient at directing war in accordance with its laws. By the line and policies, the strategy and tactics he formulated for the people's war, he led the Chinese people in steering the ship of the people's war past all hidden reefs to the shores of victory in most complicated and difficult conditions.

It must be emphasized that Comrade Mao Tse-tung's theory of the establishment of rural revolutionary base areas and the encirclement of the cities from the countryside is of outstanding and universal practical importance for the present revolutionary struggles of all the oppressed nations and peoples, and particularly for the revolutionary struggles of the oppressed nations and peoples in Asia, Africa, and Latin America against imperialism and its lackeys.

Many countries and peoples in Asia, Africa, and Latin America are now being subjected to aggression and enslavement on a serious scale by the imperialists headed by the United States and their lackeys. The basic political and economic conditions in many of these countries have many similarities to those that prevailed in old China. As in China, the peasant question is extremely important in these regions. The peasants constitute the main force of the national-democratic revolution against the imperialists and their lackeys. In committing aggression against these countries, the imperialists usually begin by seizing the big cities and the main lines of communication, but they are unable to bring the vast countryside completely under their control. The countryside, and the countryside alone, can provide the broad areas in which the revolutionaries can manoeuvre freely. The countryside, and the countryside alone, can provide the revolutionary bases from which the revolutionaries can go forward to final victory. Precisely for this reason, Comrade Mao Tse-tung's theory of establishing revolutionary base areas in the rural districts and encircling the cities from the countryside is attracting more and more attention among the people in these regions.

Taking the entire globe, if North America and Western Europe can be called "the cities of the world," then Asia, Africa and Latin America constitute "the rural areas of the world." Since World War II, the proletarian revolutionary movement has for various reasons been temporarily held back in the North American and West European capitalist countries, while the people's revolutionary movement in Asia, Africa and Latin America has been growing vigorously. In a sense, the contemporary world revolution also presents a picture of the encirclement of cities by the rural areas. In the final analysis, the whole cause of world revolution hinges on the revolutionary struggles of the Asian, African and Latin American peoples who make up the overwhelming majority of the world's population. The socialist countries should regard it as their internationalist duty to support the people's revolutionary struggles in Asia, Africa, and Latin America.

The October Revolution opened up a new era in the revolution of the oppressed nations. The victory of the October Revolution built a bridge between the socialist revolution of the proletariat of the West and the national-democratic revolution of the colonial and semi-colonial countries of the East. The Chinese revolution has successfully solved the problem of how to link up the national-democratic with the socialist revolution in the colonial and semi-colonial countries.

Comrade Mao Tse-tung has pointed out that, in the epoch since the October Revolution, anti-imperialist revolution in any colonial and semi-colonial country is no longer part of the old bourgeois, or capitalist world revolution, but is part of the new world revolution, the proletarian-socialist world revolution.

Comrade Mao Tse-tung has formulated a complete theory of the new-democratic revolution. He indicated that this revolution, which is different from all others, can only be, nay must be, a revolution against imperialism, feudalism and bureaucrat-capitalism waged by the broad masses of the people under the leadership of the proletariat.

This means that the revolution can only be, nay must be, led by the proletariat and the genuinely revolutionary party armed with Marxism-Leninism, and by no other class or party.

This means that the revolution embraces in its ranks not only the workers, peasants and the urban petty bourgeoisie, but also the national bourgeoisie and other patriotic and anti-imperialist democrats.

This means, finally, that the revolution is directed against imperialism, feudalism and bureaucrat-capitalism.

The new-democratic revolution leads to socialism, and not to capitalism.

Comrade Mao Tse-tung's theory of the new-democratic revolution is the Marxist-Leninist theory of revolution by stages as well as the Marxist-Leninist theory of uninterrupted revolution.

# 10

## A. Doak Barnett's Criticism of Mao's Mass Line[1]

*Professor A. Doak Barnett has served in the State Department and on the staff of the Ford Foundation and is now Professor of Government at Columbia University. He is the author of many books and essays on China.*

One of the most striking and distinctive aspects of the operation of the regime in China today is its continued reliance, seventeen years after coming to power, upon mass campaigns, rather than on more routinized administrative methods, to carry out its major policies and programs. This revolutionary mode of operation was clearly a product of the techniques for mass mobilization developed by the Chinese Communists during their struggle for power and during the early years of class struggle when they consolidated their power. In essence, the campaign approach to policy implementation, which grows out of their commitment to what is called the "mass line," involves the setting of a few clearly defined immediate aims, the concentration of efforts and attention on these aims above all others, the mobilization and training of large numbers of cadres drawn from many segments of the political system to carry out a campaign, and finally the mass mobilization of the population as a whole to take action to achieve the defined goals. Such campaigns rest on the premise that the masses, if they are properly organized and infused with ideological fervor, can be activated to achieve most of the society's fundamental goals, even in a modernizing society. Human will and labor, rather than technical

[1] From A. Doak Barnett, *Cadres, Bureaucracy, and Political Power in Communist China* (New York, 1967), pp. 437–38. Reprinted by permission of Columbia University Press.

**139**

skills, are seen as the key ingredients of social progress. And it is the Party itself, rather than governmental or other institutions, which generally assumes prime responsibilities for directing these campaigns.

While the effectiveness of mass campaigns during the early years of revolutionary struggle in China was indisputable, their suitability in developed society is less clear. They do have some definite advantages. They enable Communist China's leaders to concentrate their efforts at any particular time on defined objectives and to mobilize tremendous numbers of people to work toward them. However, there is little doubt that in many respects they are costly and wasteful of time and effort; they often result in the neglect of nonpriority tasks; they frequently result in the misuse of the limited reservoir of specialized talent that the country possesses; they appear to have a built-in tendency toward political excess; and they are often extremely disruptive of more regularized and routinized governmental functions. This last effect is doubtless seen by Communist China's present leaders as an asset rather than a liability, however. In fact, their persistence in using revolutionary techniques of mass mobilization is obviously motivated in part by a conscious determination to combat routinization of government, which they fear will reinforce tendencies toward increased bureaucratization, a loss of revolutionary fervor on the part of China's cadres, the reemergence of "bourgeois" value, the growth of "revisionism," and a general erosion of revolutionary momentum. In actual fact, these tendencies have steadily developed in Communist China, and as a consequence it has become increasingly difficult for Peking's leaders to mobilize the population in mass campaigns as it did in earlier years. But this appears to have reinforced their determination to try. It remains to be seen, however, how long this revolutionary method of resisting routinization and bureaucratization can be effectively pursued—particularly after a generational change in leadership occurs—and in fact one can question whether the regime will be able, over the long run, really to advance toward many of its goals of modernization without a higher degree of routinization than at present, even if the cost of routinization is increased bureaucratization and a slacking of revolutionary fervor. One can expect, therefore, a continuing dialectical interaction in Communist China between the efforts of many of the regime's leaders to promote the "mass line" and the steady growth of tendencies toward routinization and bureaucratization.

# 11

# Takeuchi Minoru on
# a Poem by Mao[1]

*Takeuchi Minoru is Professor of Chinese Literature at Toritsu University, Tokyo, and a well-known writer on Chinese literature and intellectual history.*

An unpublished poem by Mao has been brought to light by Mr. Suganuma Masahisa (member of social science delegation and fellow of the Trade Unions Research Institute) who visited China at the end of last year.

This was copied down by him when he discovered it as it was written and displayed in the lounge of the Glory old people's home at Tz'up'ing, in the heart of the Chingkang Mountains where Mao established his first base in 1927. Perhaps from a desire to give the poem more polish, its author may not commit it to print himself, but I should like to take advantage of the good offices of Mr. Suganuma and give it some kind of introduction now.

## IRREGULAR EXPRESSION USED

The poem is simple and the author's ideas can be grasped on a first reading, . . .

According to the rhyme scheme, *pu ch'ing chu*[2] in the ninth line should end in a character with the rhyme *-an*, but since Mr. Suganuma states that he too noticed this while making his copy, it cannot be his error. Mao Tse-tung is not always fastidious in ob-

---

[1] From "A Strong Will within Simplicity—seen in a recent unpublished poem," *Asahi Shimbun* (evening edition), January 19, 1967; translated by Professor P. G. O'Neill. Reprinted by permission of *Asahi Shimbun*.

[2] My English translation of this poem is on pp. 112–13, where I read *pu ch'ing chu* as *pu ch'ing k'an* (do not look down). *Chu* and *k'an* look alike, and thus are easily confused, especially if they are written in cursive script. If the character in question is read *k'an*, it does give the rhyme as Professor Takeuchi says.

serving the conventions governing this type of poem, and here he may just have said what he wanted to say, regardless of the irregularity.

Mr. Suganuma describes how the photographs of Mao displayed beside the poem show him going around looking attentively at the precipitous places of the Chingkang Mountains one after another. In that case, is it perhaps his view after his inspection that is being stated here? Even so, if it is the original text, one cannot help feeling that the words show a lack of deep thought.

In the second line of the second stanza, *ch'iang ch'i*[3] (the strong flag) probably refers to "the red flag" and is acceptable enough as an expression. . . . My feeling is that the defenses set out all around Chingkangshan and the completeness of the organization of the Red Army are being referred to here, but *huan* [in the following line] means "the earth, the globe" and is not normally used as a verb.[4]

## A MIND OF ELEGANT SIMPLICITY AND MATURITY

The poet is fond of the traditional form of poetry known as *tz'u* which is written to fixed patterns, and the *shui tiao ko t'ou* in the heading is the name of one among more than 2,000 patterns of this type of poetry. It is not the title. Under this same name he has composed a poem about his swimming across the Yangtze. It does not matter whether the name of the pattern and the content of the poem correspond or not. It could be, perhaps, that the author was attracted by the idea of using the same form for poems on both "water" and "mountains." [5]

His last published poem, in the *man chiang hung* pattern, is dated January 1963. Profound in meaning and difficult to interpret, its feeling of tension comes over very strongly.

With the present poem, this is far from the case. It is clear and serene, and unexpected in showing what one is tempted to describe

---

[3] *Ch'iang* may be either a misprint or a misreading of *ching* (banner, standard). I take the liberty to read it as *ching*, to avoid what Professor Takeuchi calls "irregularity."

[4] In my translation, *huan* is rendered as "realm."

[5] To develop this delightful point a little further, we might recall a remark by Confucius—"The kind loves mountains whereas the wise loves waters."

as a mind of elegant simplicity and maturity. I had in fact expected
a more serious work, linked up with the Cultural Revolution. The
last two lines, for example, are decidedly optimistic.

According to Mr. Suganuma, the photographs of Mao during his
visit to Chingkangshan show him completely relaxed and free in
his manner, immersed in remembrance of the past and in simple
pleasure. This would be the same kind of feeling as we experience
when we go back to homes in the country and remember our childhood days, and the poses in the photographs too were not of the
official kind which we find so often.

That being so, the impression gained from the poem is probably
accurate enough in itself. The "tall tree" in the poem is where Chu
Teh and Mao often rested when they were carrying provisions up
from the lower slopes of the mountains. Meeting this tree again,
Mao is said to have needed no prompting to give its story and a
stream of reminiscences.

It might have been better as a poem, I feel, if it had had somewhat more movement from one line to the next, but the earlier
composition of the same fixed pattern [the one on swimming—ED.]
was also of this kind. It is only natural that a figure who travelled
the whole course of a revolution should not be shut out entirely
even from a composition which is simple and serene, but one is
made aware of his strength of will whether one expects to find it
there or not.

Judging from the usage found in recent Chinese slogans, the
character *k'en* in the last line, meaning "consent (having been
asked)," [6] should certainly have been *kan* "be bold"; but this is not
to say that it is negative or passive. When about to start some new
undertaking, the poet has long had a habit of saying "Events press
in on a person," that is, "I do not do this from choice."

### PRIDE IN THE STRENGTH OF THE REVOLUTION

It is usual, however, for Mao's journeys to have some political
significance. Before the people's communes got off the mark, he
stayed in Honan for a month, and before the Cultural Revolution
he left Peking and was not easily to be seen. When we consider the

[6] In my translation, this character becomes "will."

story of how Mao confronted P'eng Teh-huai, his comrade from Chingkangshan days, at the Lushan plenum in July 1959 and, with tears in his eyes, declared: "I shall go out into the villages and begin again, with the reorganizing of another Red Army," we can see that even this visit to Chingkangshan is probably not a simple nostalgic journey, but is significant as an expression of pride at the strength of the revolution at its orginal site where, as he says with deliberate irregularity in his poem, "the dangerous places have not been brought low." [7]

[7] The corresponding line in my translation reads: "Do not look down the precipices."

# 12

# Soviet Leaders on Mao

*The sequence of events leading up to this speech is worth mentioning. On June 17, the Chinese delegation en route to the Third Congress of the Rumanian Communist Party called on Khrushchev in Moscow; on the next day, Khrushchev announced his intention to attend the Congress himself; on the 21st, the Russian delegation circulated a letter to all other delegations at Bucharest, sharply attacking China on such issues as peaceful transition to socialism, peaceful co-existence, and war and peace; on the 25th, following the Congress, the private meeting called by the Russians was in session at which many spokesmen stiffly criticized China; on the 26th, the Chinese delegation replied to the charges and at the same time circulated an earlier* private *letter from the CPSU to the CCP; and on the 27th, Khrushchev spoke.*

### N. KHRUSHCHEV AT THE BUCHAREST CONFERENCE, June 7, 1960—A SPEECH SUMMARIZED BY EDWARD CRANKSHAW [1]

He [Khrushchev] attacked Mao Tse-tung by name, saying that he was in fact another Stalin, "oblivious of any interests other than his own, spinning theories detached from the realities of the modern world." He had become "an ultra Leftist, an ultra dogmatist, indeed, a *left revisionist.*" The Chinese, he said, talked a great deal about war, but in fact they simply did not understand the meaning of modern war. He had a great deal to say about the frontier dispute with India, rejecting violently the Chinese charge that the Russians had let them down by refusing to support them. In fact,

[1] From Edward Crankshaw, *The New Cold War Moscow v. Peking* (Middlesex, 1963), pp. 107–9. Reprinted by permission of A. D. Peters & Co.

it had been the Chinese who had let the cause of Socialism down. By quarrelling with the Government of India they had not merely failed to work with the Russians towards the socialization of India; they had worked against it. Of course Nehru was a capitalist. But the Chinese dispute with him had nothing to do with capitalism and Socialism: it was a purely nationalist dispute and it had done the Socialist cause untold harm, quite apart from such details as losing Kerala to Communism. What right had Peng [Chen] to complain of lack of support in such circumstances, especially when anyway it was impossible to get at the rights and wrongs of the dispute? Why, moreover, should the Chinese, who are always boasting of their colossal population, need support from the Soviet Union, whose population was less than the population of India? And what would happen to this frontier dispute when the day came, as it would, when India was a Socialist country? The Chinese comrades, he said, should take to heart what Lenin had said about great nation chauvinism. They should also remember that it had been Lenin who was prepared to surrender territory for tactical reasons —as under the Treaty of Brest Litovsk—and Trotsky who had opposed any abandonment of territory. Meanwhile Nehru had become a national hero, and this was just what the imperialists desired. The Soviet Union too had her frontier problems. But she approached these in a responsible way. If she had taken the Chinese line, war would have been declared on Iran more than once. There had been plenty of border incidents on the Russo-Iranian frontier, and men had been killed in them. But the Soviet Union would not allow incidents of this kind to precipitate war, since this would contradict the true spirit of revolution.

He attacked the Chinese for calling in question the whole attack on the personality cult. He lifted a small corner of the veil over Sino-Soviet military cooperation when he complained bitterly that the Chinese had hampered Soviet defence measures on the Manchurian border by preventing the installation of a radio transmitter "for use against our enemies" and hindering reconnaissance flights by Soviet aircraft.

But his greatest contempt and bitterness was reserved for Chinese methods of controversy and Chinese domestic expedients. The Chinese were trying to force their views on others, he said. The methods they used in the matter of the W.F.T.U. were purely Trot-skyite in kind. And yet they "sent Peng Teh-huai to a labour camp" because he had dared criticize the policy of the communes in a letter to the C.P.S.U. The Russians did not agree with the communes, nor with the Great Leap Forward. But they had not said so. They thought the "Hundred Flowers" policy had been mistaken. But they had not said so. Development of a country's economy had to be regular, not in leaps and bounds. He added, interestingly, that strikes had occurred in Russia as a result of trying to force the pace.

### LEONID ILYICHEV, "REVOLUTIONARY SCIENCE AND OUR AGE: AGAINST THE ANTI-LENINIST COURSE OF THE CHINESE LEADERS" (July, 1964)[2]

*Written by the head of the Agitprop section of the Central Committee of the CPSU, this article was released to the Russian press on July 31 and published in English on October 1, 1964, a mere fortnight before the removal of N. Khrushchev as First Secretary and Chairman of the Council of Ministers. At a time when the deterioration of Sino-Soviet relations was almost beyond repair, Ilyichev articulated the Russian position on one of the greatest controversies in the history of the International Communist Movement.*

The ideology of the personality cult runs counter to the very spirit of Leninism, to the nature of the revolutionary working-class movement and of the socialist system. The practice of concentrating all power in the hands of a single individual is alien to the nature of the proletarian state, to the principles of socialist democracy. It is especially baneful in a country still weighted down by the unpleasant "burden" of such survivals of the feudal past as worship of the monarch, domination of a hierarchy and omnipotence of bureaucracy.

[2] From *Kommunist*, No. 11 (1964), pp. 12–35, in *Information Bulletin*, No. 21 (October 1, 1964).

The cult of Mao Tse-tung's personality could not but lead in China to distortions of the socialist principles of state and Party development and of the democratic forms and methods of administration.

For 20 years prior to the victory of the revolution, all ideological and organizational work in the Communist Party of China was conducted along military lines, subordinated to wartime needs. For that period this procedure evidently was justified. But 15 years have already passed since the end of hostilities. With the switchover to peaceful work, have the Chinese leaders taken any measures to change the Party's style of work, to promote democratic centralism? No, they have not. The army style, based on one-man command, on unquestioning obedience to orders from above, has remained the basis of Party activity. Moreover, militarization of all aspects of social life has been intensified in recent years. As before, criticism and other elementary standards of inner-party democracy are lacking.

True, at one time after the 20th Congress of the CPSU, the Chinese leadership began to speak about developing democracy. But that is as far as it went.

An extensive campaign is now being conducted in China under the slogan: "Learn to work like the People's Liberation Army." Political bodies patterned after the army political departments are being set up in the entire system of the Party, state and economic apparatus of China, from the Central Committee of the CCP down to enterprises and communes. Mao Tse-tung has declared: "All our economic branches, branches of industry, agriculture and trade must study the methods of the People's Liberation Army, must organize and intensify political work. Only in this way will it be possible to arouse the revolutionary spirit of millions and tens of millions of personnel and the masses on the entire economic front." (*Hung Ch'i*, 1964, no. 6)

Note, it is not the army that has to learn from the Party, but the Party from the army. In other words, the accent is on the army and the principles of army discipline, while the Leninist teaching on the Party is discarded.

What should be learned from the army? Party organizations of

China are given the following directive: Communists must learn from the army "to carry out orders resolutely, swiftly and strictly, without entering into arguments and without haggling—do what you are ordered." (*Jen-min Jih-pao*, February 1, 1964) How can one speak of Party democracy when all that is demanded of a Party member is blind obedience. The demand that you unquestioningly carry out orders and, moreover, pretend that this is inner-party democracy, is sheer blasphemy. This is how the elementary standards of Party life are violated, criticism from below and the creative activity of Communists crushed, how informing and servility are encouraged. The Political Bureau of the Central Committee of the Communist Party of China and Mao Tse-tung who, judging from his directive, only issue orders, consider themselves to be exempt from Party control, from control of the Party members.

The atmosphere created by the personality cult cannot but lead to a situation when subjectivism and the personal whims of one man become an official policy, create fertile soil for unjustified experiments, absence of control, inordinate ambition, make for extremes, instability, adventurism, and nationalism. It is in this atmosphere that the nationalist, left opportunist, neo-Trotskyite deviation has made its nest.

### PRAVDA ON THE RENEGADES FROM MARXISM (February 16, 1967)[3]

The entire practice of the CPSU and the other communist parties, which are consistently developing the Leninist intra-party norms, strengthening principles of collective leadership, and adhering strictly to democratic principles in the activities of all party organizations from top to bottom, naturally creates a danger to Mao Tse-tung and his power. For Mao Tse-tung's group has long been attacking its own party. The most elementary norms and principles of inner party life—electivity of party bodies, responsibility of leaders to the party and party organizations, publicity in the discussion of the party line, etc., have been trampled underfoot in China. Mao Tse-tung's personality cult has reached the absurd,

[3] From *Survey*, London, April, 1967, pp. 39–40. Reprinted by permission of *Survey*.

has become real idolatry. The routing of party organizations, the hounding and annihilation of party cadres is in full swing under the flag of the "cultural revolution," and is being carried out by detachments of Mao Tse-tung's storm troopers with the support of the army and security service. In order to justify all this and in order to muzzle the Chinese communists who cannot but compare the things happening in China with the practice of other communist parties, the Mao Tse-tung group had to smear the CPSU's Leninist line and to level the absurd charge of "revisionism" against it.

The history of the working class movement demonstrates that renegades from Marxism have always shown blind hatred for the banner which they had betrayed. The Mao Tse-tung group is not an exception in this respect. One of the main tasks of the anti-Soviet hysteria it is now fanning is to fence the Chinese people off from genuine Marxism-Leninism, from the experience of world socialism. In the present conditions this experience is not only alien to the Chinese leaders but is dangerous to them, because knowledge of this experience would only show the communist party and people of China how far their leaders had departed from the interests of the revolution and socialism. That is why the Chinese leadership had to isolate their country, to erect a "Chinese wall" to keep their people away from the socialist community, from the entire progressive world public . . . Mao Tse-tung's erroneous policy has led the country into an impasse. Seeing no way out, the Chinese leadership rushes from one adventure to another. Its anti-Sovietism is precisely one such adventure.


### L. BREZHNEV ON THE CULTURAL REVOLUTION [4]

*This speech was given at a rally in Budapest after the signing of the Treaty of Friendship, Co-operation, and Mutual Assistance between the USSR and Hungary. Janos Kadar, the Hungarian Communist leader, also spoke, and he declared: "The Hungarian socialist Workers' Party most categorically*

---

[4] From a speech in Budapest on September 7, 1967, BBC *Summary of World Broadcasts*, EE/2564/C/11–12. Reprinted by permission of The British Broadcasting Corporation.

*rejects Mao Tse-tung's policy which greatly harms the inter-
ests of the Chinese people, the peoples of the socialist countries, and the International Communist Movement."*

The latest events in China show that Mao Tse-tung and his
followers are jeopardizing the Chinese people's revolutionary gains.
What is termed by Mao Tse-tung's group the "cultural revolution"
should be more correctly called a counter-revolution. The people's
democratic power is in fact being threatened in China today. The
established bodies of the Party and the constitutional bodies of
State power have actually ceased their activities. The trade unions,
the Youth League, and public organizations have been dissolved.
Many prominent and esteemed Party and Government leaders,
well-known participants in the Chinese revolution, outstanding
military commanders, major representatives of culture and science,
are being defamed and subjected to inhuman repression.

The social gains and rights of the working people are being reduced to nothing. The Chinese workers and peasants who, in various parts of the country, are opposing the arbitrariness of Mao
Tse-tung and his henchmen are being suppressed by force of arms.
Not only groups of fanatical Red Guards and rebels who are blinded
by false propaganda, but also deceived army units are being sent
against the workers and peasants. But in the army itself an ever
growing number of soldiers and officers are beginning to understand for what aims Mao Tse-tung's group is trying to use them.
The events in China show not only the ideological and political
bankruptcy of Mao Tse-tung's group but also the strength of the
resistance to this policy from broad sections of the working people,
numerous Party and Government cadres, and the best representatives of the armed forces.

The Communist Party and people of China are now living
through a critical period in their history. But no matter how complicated the struggle will be, we are convinced that ultimately they
will find sufficient strength in themselves to uphold the gains of
the revolution and lead their country to the correct path. We are
convinced that in the long run the cause of socialism in China will
win. The CPSU and the entire Soviet people, whose attitude to the

Communist Party and people of China is invariably imbued with a spirit of fraternal friendship and proletarian internationalism, will welcome this as an important victory of our common great cause.

# PART THREE

# MAO IN HISTORY

> *As Mao is still alive and his career as a revolutionary and ruler of China has not yet ended, assessment of him as an historical figure is premature. Very few scholars have even hinted at what Mao's place in history is likely to be. Here Professors Maurice Meisner and Stuart Schram describe the origins and characteristics of Mao's thought and evaluate his contribution to Marxism-Leninism. Following their statements is my own appraisal of his contribution as a revolutionary.*

## Maurice Meisner on Activism and Voluntarism[1]

> *Maurice Meisner is Associate Professor of history at the University of Virginia and fellow at the Center for Advanced Study in the Behavioral Sciences at Stanford, California.*

Both Li [Ta-chao] and Mao felt the need to find objective Marxist correlatives for what was basically a subjective system of revolutionary values, and both drew from the materialist conception of history the assurance of the inevitability of socialism. But their socialist faith was ultimately based not upon confidence in the workings of the objective laws of social development, but rather upon confidence in their abilities to bring forth the powerful subjective forces latent in the present—the great storehouses of "surplus energy" that Li argued had been accumulating in China over

---

[1] From Maurice Meisner, *Li Ta-chao and the Origins of Chinese Marxism* (Cambridge, Mass., 1967), pp. 263–64. Copyright © 1967 by the President and Fellows of Harvard College. Reprinted by permission of Harvard University Press.

**154**

the centuries. The ideas, the wills, and the "self-consciousness" of men would really determine the course of Chinese history.

These activistic and voluntaristic impulses were inspired by and also reinforced even more deeply rooted nationalistic impulses. For Mao, as well as for Li, the salvation and rebirth of the Chinese nation was the major concern, but it was to be a socialist rebirth, China's precapitalist social and economic structure notwithstanding, for China was not to be allowed to fall behind in the progressive march of history. It was to achieve this rebirth that both undertook to transform Marxist doctrine. In the process of the transformation the internationalist and cosmopolitan content of the original doctrine gave way to a messianic nationalism, which saw China not only fully qualified to join the forces of international socialism but destined to play a special role in the world revolution.

The combination of revolutionary voluntarism and Chinese nationalism made for a curious dichotomy in both Li's and Mao's vision of the rebirth of China. Although their confidence in this rebirth was based upon their faith in the energies of the people, particularly the youth, who were to write a new Chinese history in accordance with the new Marxist ideals and values which had come from the West, this very real rejection of the values of old China was accompanied by a nationalistic attachment to Chinese traditions and a feeling of pride in the glories of the Chinese past.

The combination of voluntarism and nationalism was also reflected in their treatment of the concept of class struggle, the theoretical area most directly related to political practice. Both Li and Mao promoted class struggle in theory as well as in practice. However, they drew from Marx's theory more the notion of struggle than the need to analyze political situations upon the basis of objective social class criteria. "Proletarian consciousness" was more important than the proletariat itself. Li was quite explicit in attributing a latent proletarian consciousness to the entire Chinese nation by virtue of China's "proletarian" status in the international capitalist economy, and this idea was implicit in Mao's thesis that the major contest was not so much within China as between the Chinese nation and foreign imperialism. These notions reflected not only the voluntarist's impatience with the economic forces of history and his impulse to carry out the proletarian revolution, even without the actual proletariat if need be, but also the willingness of the Chinese nationalist to abandon the only progressive social class in Chinese society that had been formed in the image of the West and instead look to broader, "national" sources of revolution.

# Stuart Schram on the Origins and Characteristics of Mao's Thought[2]

*Having taken his Ph.D. at Columbia University, Professor Stuart Schram worked at the Centre d'Étude des Relations Internationales in Paris before taking up the directorship of the Contemporary China Institute at the University of London.*

Mao's debt to Lenin is obvious. He owes him the conception that political consciousness does not manifest itself spontaneously among the proletariat but must be instilled by an elite or vanguard—the Party. He also is indebted to him for the theory and practice of Party organization in accordance with the principles of "democratic centralism." He owes him the theory of "imperialism," which explains how normally hostile classes in dependent societies are united by a common interest in opposing foreign exploitation; he owes him also the idea of an alliance between the proletariat and certain other classes, particularly the peasantry, as the form of state power during the "democratic" (i.e. presocialist) phase of the revolution. And to Lenin's disciple, Stalin, he owes the formula of the "four-class bloc" (workers, peasants, petty bourgeoisie, and national bourgeoisie), which lies at the heart of his theory of "people's democratic dictatorship."

And yet, though much of this Leninist and Stalinist heritage is still apparent in Mao-Tse-tung's thought, it has been transformed into something which is not only different but which has its own characteristic unity. If Lenin arbitrarily identified the Communist Party with the true will of the real proletariat, Mao and his friends affirm that the Party can substitute itself for a virtually nonexistent

[2] From Stuart Schram, *The Political Thought of Mao Tse-Tung* (London, 1964; New York, 1963), pp. 78–80. Reprinted by permission of Pall Mall Press and Frederick A. Praeger, Inc.

157

proletariat as the leader of the agrarian revolution. If Lenin laid down the basic principles of Party organization adhered to by Communists in all countries, Mao (and even more Liu Shao-ch'i) have supplemented these with ideals of self-cultivation of Party members, which owe as much to the Confucian tradition as to Marx. If Lenin not only developed the general theory of imperialism, but went very far, especially at the Second Comintern Congress, in spelling out the detailed tactics of collaboration with "bourgeois" nationalists to be applied by Communists in colonial and semi-colonial areas, the fact remains that for him all such compromises with nationalism were dictated by necessity rather than by choice. Lenin was a European primarily interested in world revolution, who regarded the very existence of national differences as a misfortune, though as a realist he was quite prepared to compromise with nationalism if in this way he could harness the revolutionary energies of the colonial countries to his larger goal. Mao, on the other hand, is an Asian for whom nationalism is not a necessary evil but an authentic value in itself. Out of this grows his use of formulas such as that of the four-class bloc, which for Stalin was a mere passing phase in the development of the revolution, whereas in Mao's view it is possible to go all the way to Communism under the joint dictatorship of the workers, peasants, petty bourgeoisie, and national bourgeoisie—even if some of these components are more equal than others.

There is abroad today, as the principal alternative to Communism in the underdeveloped countries, a type of ideology that might be described succinctly as "Leninism minus the class struggle." The adherents of such theories accept Lenin's diagnosis of the role of Western imperialism in the non-European countries, but reject the class struggle in favor of national solidarity. In a sense, this type of "populist" nationalism offers a more realistic program of action in nations where class lines are fuzzy and traditional Marxist stereotypes do not seem to apply. But it also suffers from a serious weakness as compared to more orthodox Leninist views, for in throwing out the class struggle it also throws out the only theoretical justification for the leading role of the governing party, apart from the subjective sense of mission of certain charismatic leaders. And it also sacrifices the principle of "proletarian internationalism," which, while more honored in the breach than in the observance (except as a mere disguise for Russian national interest in Stalin's day), at least offers a reminder that the ultimate goals of human society cannot be defined simply in terms of the preservation of certain national entities and their presumed unique virtues. Perhaps the best brief characterization of Mao's thought would be to say that, while still remaining technically an orthodox Leninist, he has succeeded to a considerable extent in incorporating the values and appeals of "populist" nationalism. On the one hand, he maintains that only the proletariat can carry out a genuine revolution. On the other, he reserves for the bourgeoisie a place among the "people." He affirms that without a leader, the forces of the international Communist movement may disintegrate and at the same time proclaims loudly that the Chinese Communist Party will consider itself bound by no declarations or agreements that it has not accepted of its own free will.

Apart from the populist strain in his thought and the immense role of the peasantry in his rise to power, Mao's contribution to the theory and practice of revolution is also characterized by an extreme voluntarism. To be sure, "voluntarism," in the sense of an accent on conscious action, is by no means absent from Marx himself. But there is no doubt that it is carried much further in Lenin, and further still in Mao Tse-tung, and in the ideology of the Chinese Communist Party. This voluntarism attains a kind of apotheosis in the theory of the permanent revolution. Consider, for example, a passage such as this:

> Men are not the slaves of objective reality. Provided only that men's consciousness be in conformity with the objective laws of the development of things, the subjective activity of the popular masses can manifest itself in full measure, overcome all difficulties, create the necessary conditions, and carry forward the revolution. In this sense, *the subjective creates the objective.* [Italics added.]

As emphasized previously, Lenin opened the door to this kind of development with his theory that in periods of revolution, politics takes precedence over economics. But there is no doubt that here the Chinese Communists carry this trend a step further, a step that

Lenin would have refused to take. One of the roots of this tendency in Chinese Communist ideology is unquestionably the situation of China as an underdeveloped country, which has engendered a mood of impatience, a desire to transform the environment overnight. But in Mao's case this situational factor has been tremendously reinforced by his love of struggle and drama.

# Stuart Schram on
# Mao's Contribution
# to Dialectics[3]

Where is Mao's real contribution to "dialectics" to be found? He has added little of importance to the laws or concepts of Marxist philosophy. But he has brought to the solution of political problems—and to the political applications of philosophy —a mind which sees reality as a ceaseless flux extending to infinity. In his view, man and society will be re-shaped in a never-ending process of struggle which will continue even after full communism has been established.

It is this mentality which infuses the theory of "permanent" or "uninterrupted" revolution. . . . It is a mentality which is the opposite of the bureaucratic mentality which marks the communist parties of the Soviet Union and of most European countries. At its best, it is a surprisingly open-minded mentality, and this open-mindedness is directly linked to the dialectical character of Mao's thought, which sees in everything, including Marx and Mao himself, merely a provisional contribution to be subsumed in some higher synthesis. At its worst, as it appears today, it is a primitive and militarist mentality, impatient with reality when it fails to bend to the will of the leader. These contradictory tendencies are inextricably mingled in Mao's thought and action. They are clearly visible in the China of the Red Guards, which endeavours to achieve the ultimate in regimentation through the ultimate in spontaneity, and to combine the uncritical worship of the leader with the ideology of uninterrupted "revolt."

[3] From the *China Quarterly*, No. 29 (January–March, 1967), pp. 164–65. Reprinted by permission of *China Quarterly*.

# Jerome Ch'en on Mao's Role in Chinese History [4]

Although he embraced Marxism as early as 1919 when he was twenty-six, he did not take up arms against the authorities until 1927. For twenty-two years he fought relentlessly, through the defeat in 1934–5, the Long March, the United Front, and the civil war, to his final victory. The sustaining power is partly due to the malevolence of the KMT persecution and partly to the hatred which is so essential a part of Mao's personality.

Some attribute the intensity of Mao's hatred to the harsh treatment he suffered at the hands of his father, others suggest that it was aroused by his early reading of such novels as *The Water Margin (Shui Hu)*. I think rather that its origin is to be found in his reading of Darwin, Rousseau, J. S. Mill, and F. Paulsen, which broadened his vision and encouraged him to break away from obsolete tradition. Revolutionary literature by anarchists and Marxists later suggested how the emancipation of his nation could be achieved. His own experience and observation of injustice, poverty, and incessant civil war further increased his indignation. There can be no other rational explanation of his persistent hatred. No one can sustain such hatred without continually seeking a way to end it. Thus Mao's hatred sharpened his vision and enabled him to see beyond the thing he hated so much a new China, the China he wanted to create, which would be independent, free, peaceful, united, and above all, strong and prosperous.

> The Chinese people will see that, once China's destiny is in the hands of the people, China, like the sun rising in the east, will illuminate every corner of the land with a brilliant flame, swiftly clean up the mire left by the reactionary government, heal the wounds of war and build a new, powerful and prosperous people's republic worthy of the name.

[4] From Jerome Ch'en, *Mao and the Chinese Revolution* (London, New York, 1965), pp. 6–8. Reprinted by permission of Oxford University Press.

Or:

*once the cock has crowed and all beneath the sky is bright.*

This is nothing new. The demand for a powerful and prosperous China had been voiced in the 1860's and throughout the ensuing decades. The difference lay in the means whereby strength and prosperity were to be achieved. The earliest leaders of the self-strengthening movement prescribed the modernization of China's defence—"strong warships and efficient guns"; the second generation added economic wealth to the recipe. Then came the Sino-Japanese War of 1894–5 and China's ignominious defeat which utterly discredited the self-strengthening policies. What remained unchanged, however, were the ultimate aims of these policies. The third generation gave priority to an administrative reform, aiming at the transformation of China's autocracy into a constitutional monarchy; this, too, failed. Representing the fourth generation, Dr. Sun Yat-sen and Chiang Kai-shek led their revolutions in 1911 and 1926–8 by which they hoped to establish a republic which would at the same time be democratic and conform to the Confucian tradition. Coming to power after the Russian Revolution and at the time of the world economic depression, Chiang's policies were constantly interrupted by civil wars, the communist challenge, and the Japanese aggression. The defeat of Japan with the help of the Allies in 1945 meant that China, for the first time in fifty years, was free from the haunting shadow of her aggressive neighbour, but by that time the "spectre of communism" had grown to such a menacing size that neither Chiang's military strength nor his will power was enough to exercise it. Chiang's departure and Mao's inauguration did not mean a change in the immediate aims of China's policies, for what Mao wanted in 1949, as he still does now, was a powerful and prosperous country. In this sense Mao represents a new generation of the century-long self-strengthening movement.

Parallel to the development of the self-strengthening movement was the under-current of China's peasant movement, beginning in the recent past with the T'aip'ing Rebellion, which ravaged the southern half of China for fourteen years, and continuing with the

Nien Rebels and the Boxers in the closing decades of the nineteenth century. All these rebels distrusted the Government's ability to fulfil its promise of a strong and prosperous China. The T'aip'ings and the Niens wanted to overthrow the Manchu régime and replace it with one of their own, in order to end social injustice and put the country on a more solid basis; the Boxers, believing in magic powers, tried to oust foreign influence in China. These rebels followed the traditional pattern of the peasant revolt, a protracted military struggle from one or several base areas with the poor peasants as their main supporters. Mao also relied on the poor peasants in waging a protracted war against the authorities from one or several revolutionary bases. In this sense, Mao was the leader of a new generation of insurgent peasants.

Mao differs, however, from both the self-strengthening leaders and peasant insurgents of the past in that he is a Marxist-Leninist seeking to strengthen his country by the application of Marxist-Leninist doctrines to Chinese conditions. In his view, China could not become powerful and wealthy until she was freed from imperialist and feudal bondage. He believed that the only force strong enough to bring about her emancipation was a Marxist party supported, in theory, by urban workers and rural peasants, but, in practice, mainly by peasants, especially armed peasants. By relying on the peasantry, he is said to have Sinicized Marxism. However . . . it is by the adoption of the Chinese traditional patterns of the peasant revolt, and by developing a system of strategy and tactics around it in order to realize Marxist-Leninist aims, that he has made his greatest contribution to Marxist thinking and Sinicized communism.

# Afterword

Mao's rule of China will inevitably come to an end. What will follow that eventuality? Professor A. Doak Barnett, in his Walter E. Edge lectures delivered at Princeton University in 1967,[1] tries to answer this question by comparing Mao's personality, political style, and influence with China's needs. He sees in Mao a charismatic leader who is romantic and backward-looking because of the fascination of the past—the Yenan spirit and revolutionary success—and who is irreplaceable because of his ability to weld the party leadership together. China, in other words, is caught on the horns of Mao's unreality and unchallengeability. These attributes have led her to impose upon herself the Yenan spirit of self-sacrifice, austerity, ideological reform, and egalitarianism by means of mass mobilization and ideological indoctrination. In an age of nuclear weapons, computers, and space capsules, Barnett thinks, these efforts are antiquarian and obsolete.

Modernization presumably is the goal shared by all the leaders of China of this generation and will remain so in future. But modernization depends, according to Barnett, less upon spirit and ideology than upon organization and impersonal discipline, less upon coercion than upon incentives, less upon revolution than upon peaceful construction. Mao's insistence upon the Yenan style in order to achieve the prescribed target has led to a divergence of views between the Maoists and the pragmatists. As long as Mao is alive and authoritative, a measure of unity can be preserved within the leadership through either persuasion or purges. Yet for lack of a decisive success since the 1950's, stresses and strains remain. When Mao goes, the leadership, already shaken now by the Cultural Revolution, will become even less cohesive as various policy alternatives compete more sharply. Although the nation will bear Mao's stamp for some time to come, future generations of Chinese leaders, from their different backgrounds and experi-

[1] *China After Mao* (Princeton, N. J., 1967).

ences, will have a more flexible outlook and a more pragmatic approach to China's problems. When that day comes, Maoism will pass into history.

Is not Barnett's vision of China's future just what Mao calls revisionism and what he combats? Why is such a vision so fearsome from Mao's point of view? If revisionism is good for China, why does not Mao, as a patriot, accept it? If scholars are not prepared to doubt Mao's patriotism or to regard the Cultural Revolution simply as a power struggle, they must seek a rational explanation of his motivation and recent action. Barnett ascribes this to Mao's romanticism.

With the advantage of one more year's observation, another eminent American, Edgar Snow, faced this same question as put to him by Professor Nomura Koichi at a China Forum organized by the Japanese newspaper *Asahi Shimbun* in May 1968.[2] Snow's paradox springs from inability to reconcile his American background with his great familiarity with China. Thus, on the one hand, he admits the unsuitability of the Yenan style to modern production and, on the other, sees the necessity of the Yenan spirit (equality, friendship, comradeship, self-sacrifice, and dedication to the country) for a poor nation like China in order for her to accumulate capital and break the strangle hold of its ancient family system and bureaucracy. Without capital aid from abroad, the Chinese have to save hard for their modernization—hence the need for a revival of the Yenan spirit and for great emphasis upon what Snow calls "human engineering." Unless the Chinese themselves can be made both "*red* and expert" in the sense that they are *selflessly* and efficiently working for the wealth and power of a socialist state, China will have no future. The Russian experience of developing socialism has little bearing on China's problems; China's solution requires both a higher degree of self-sacrifice and the avoidance of bureaucratism. But Snow is not sure whether China has really solved for herself the question of unity and modernization that exists among independent countries in which the working class owns the means of production. The Chinese model, like the Russian one, is highly nationalistic in character.

Snow is not so categorical as Barnett in asserting the incom-

[2] Special edition of the *Asahi Journal,* X (1968), No. 18 (in Japanese).

patibility of Maoism and modernization. Snow's consideration of the problems of capital formation and of the growth of bureaucratism presents a more cogent explanation of Mao's motives than does Barnett's pronouncement on Mao's romanticism. In Snow's eyes, Mao is neither unrealistic nor obsolete. None the less, Snow does express a suspicion that the Yenan style may not work in harmony with modern reality. By modern reality both authors mean the successful experience of the industrialization of Europe (including Russia), America, and Japan which is characterized by the rule of law, stratified organizations, and material incentives. These successes understandably lead both of them, as well as many others, to doubt whether Mao's reliance upon the rule of virtue, egalitarian organizations, and moral incentives will be fruitful. Their doubt seems to be based upon an hypothesis—the universal applicability of what might conveniently be called the experience of the West, or more precisely its American background. The temptation to use this frame of reference when explaining or doubting Mao's deviation from it is strong and natural wherever precise information on a specific Chinese problem is lacking. Not only Barnett and Snow find this temptation hard to resist; the "moderates" in China such as Liu Shao-ch'i, Teng Hsiao-p'ing, and to some extent Chou En-lai have almost certainly shared their feeling.

Mao's main difference in this respect comes from his refusal to depend upon empirical knowledge alone. As far as he can see, Chinese problems are vastly different from those of other countries and should be tackled differently. He believes in his own visionary power and realism and is now moving heaven and earth to develop his country according to his prediction. "Without prophetic power," he once remarked, "there can be no question of leadership." He may succeed or fail. Whatever happens, when all is said and done, a man's vision and prophetic power may help to create something that will not turn out to be so new or so different as initially conceived. Still, this is how progress is made.

# Bibliographical Note

In recent years, a great deal had been published in China and elsewhere on Mao and the Chinese Communist movement, and consequently, a comprehensive bibliography, if at all possible, would take a considerable amount of time to compile and the space of a monograph to print it. This note, mainly for those who prefer to read in English, limits itself to basic treatises on these two subjects. Students may find it helpful, however, to consult *Guide to the Writings of Mao Tse-tung in the East Asiatic Library* and its *Supplement I* (published by Columbia University Libraries), *The Thought of Mao Tse-tung* (by the Department of State), and the two short lists on Mao's works by the Hoover Institution. Also published by the Hoover Institution are two volumes of annotated bibliography, *The Chinese Communist Movement 1921–1937* and *1937–1949*, compiled by Hsueh Chun-tu. Howard L. Boorman's article, "Mao Tse-tung: the lacquered image," in the *China Quarterly*, No. 16, itself a good biography, carries with it a useful bibliography.

Of Mao's own writings there are the *Selected Works* (1961–65), *Selected Readings* (1967), *Selected Military Writings* (1963), *Nineteen Poems* (1958), and *Quotations from Chairman Mao Tse-tung* (1966)—all from the Foreign Language Press, Peking.

About the man himself, Siao Yu has written *Mao Tse-tung and I Were Beggars* (London and Syracuse, 1961 and 1959) which, though historically unsound, gives some interesting insights on Mao as a student at the First Teacher's Training College in Ch'angsha. Siao's brother, Hsiao San, who was also a schoolmate of Mao, with his fulsome *Mao Tse-tung, His Childhood and Youth* (Bombay, 1953), helped to inaugurate the personality cult of Mao in the early 1940's. Another Chinese account comes from Mao's political opponent, Chang Kuo-t'ao: "Mao—a New Portrait by an Old Colleague," *New*

*York Times Magazine,* August 2, 1953. Mao's own story of his life and works up to 1936 is vividly and objectively recorded in Edgar Snow's *Red Star over China* (London, New York, 1937, 1968). A sequel to it is to be found in Snow's *Other Side of the River: Red China Today* (New York, 1962). Early in 1965, Snow visited Mao again, and their interview was published in the *Washington Post* and the *Sunday Times,* London, on February 14, 1965.

Short notes and anecdotes about Mao are included in Nym Wales, *My Yenan Notebooks* (Madison, Conn.: mimeographed, 1961) and Robert Payne, *Portrait of a Revolutionary: Mao Tse-tung* (London, 1961). The latter, because of its familiarity with neither Mao's thought nor the history of the Chinese Communist movement, has failed in its attempt to give its subject coherent treatment. Agnes Smedley's *The Great Road* (London, 1958), though not strictly on Mao, throws considerable light upon his early revolutionary activities.

Among serious studies on Mao, Benjamin Schwartz, *Chinese Communism and the Rise of Mao* (Cambridge, Mass., 1951) is a brilliant pioneer work, which analyses the emergence of Mao's deviation and contribution in their complex ideological and historical background. Also noteworthy and by far the most comprehensive is Stuart R. Schram, *Mao Tse-tung* (Middlesex, 1967). These two scholars have made important contributions to the understanding of Mao and almost anything written by them on this subject is worth reading. There is also my own work, *Mao and the Chinese Revolution* (London, 1965), which endeavors to link up Mao's life and works with the revolutionary movements in China up to 1949.

A collection of representative documents with detailed notes and comments was brought out by Conrad Brandt, Benjamin Schwartz, and John K. Fairbank under the title, *A Documentary History of Chinese Communism* (Cambridge, Mass., 1962). It serves as useful reference to all who study the movement up to the victory of the Communist revolution in 1949. A turning point in this period was known as the Rectification Campaign of 1942–44, and this is documented, though (in the

light of recent discoveries and revelations) not adequately, by
Boyd Compton—*Mao's China: Party Reform Documents
1942–1944,* edited with an introduction (Seattle, 1952). The
turbulent episode of the Socialist High Tide and the Great
Leap Forward induces another collection of documents—
*Communist China 1955–1959,* policy documents with a fore-
word by Robert R. Bowie and John K. Fairbank (Cambridge,
Mass., 1962).

Official interpretations of the Chinese Communist move-
ment are represented by Ho Kan-chih, *A History of the Modern Chinese Revolution* (Peking, 1960) and Hu Chiao-mu,
*Thirty Years of the Communist Party of China* (London,
1951). On "the other side of the river" is Chiang Kai-shek's
*Soviet Russia in China: A Summing-up at Seventy* (London,
1957). But to understand the intellectual background of the
Chinese Communist movement, one should consult Chow
Tse-tsung's monumental work *The May Fourth Movement:
Intellectual Revolution in Modern China* (Cambridge, Mass.,
1960) and follow it up with three works on the 1927–1934
period—Hsiao Tso-liang, *Power Relations within the Chinese
Communist Movement, 1930–1934* (Seattle, 1961); Shanti
Swarup, *A Study of the Chinese Communist Movement 1927–
1934* (London, 1966); and John E. Rue, *Mao Tse-tung in
Opposition 1927–1935* (Stanford, Calif., 1966). The heroics of
the Long March (1934–1936) are recorded in Snow's *Red Star*
and *The Long March: Eyewitness Accounts* and are analyzed,
to some extent, in Schram's and my biographies of Mao. *The
Long March* was published in Peking by the Foreign Language Press in 1963. Depending mainly upon Japanese ar-
chives, Chalmers A. Johnson has written *Peasant Nationalism
and Communist Power: The Emergence of Revolutionary
China 1937–1945* (Stanford, Calif., 1962), which puts forward
an interesting and largely acceptable thesis. The early years of
the People's Republic are competently dealt with in A. Doak
Barnett, *Communist China: The Early Years, 1949–1955* (New
York, 1964).

The upheavals in China from 1966 to the present may have
upset many scholars and commentators, but Franz Schur-

mann's *Ideology and Organization in Communist China* remains an important work on the subject it deals with. This is published by the University of California Press, 1966. On the leadership, there is John Wilson Lewis's *Leadership in Communist China* (Ithaca, N.Y., 1963). This, however, is a difficult subject to work on in view of the paucity of available material and in the light of the Cultural Revolution. A new work on this subject may be needed. A. Doak Barnett's recent work, *Cadres, Bureaucracy, and Political Power in Communist China* (New York, 1967), with a contribution from Jerome A. Cohen, is a fascinating study based on a series of interviews conducted in Hong Kong. To continue with background studies, one also should read *New China Economic Achievements* (Peking, 1952); Li Choh-ming, *Economic Development of Communist China* (Berkeley, Calif., 1959); Wu Yuan-li, *The Economy of Communist China: An Introduction* (New York, 1965); and the most comprehensive survey of China's planning mechanism, *China's Economic System* (London, 1967) by Audrey Donnithorne.

The coining of "Maoism" and the dispute over Mao's originality lead to Karl A. Wittfogel's corrective, "The Legend of 'Maoism,'" the *China Quarterly*, Nos. 1–2, and to Benjamin Schwartz's rejoinder "The Legend of the 'Legend of "Maoism,"'" in the same journal, No. 2. Earlier, Schwartz discussed Mao's originality in his review of the *Selected Works* —"On the 'Originality' of Mao Tse-tung," in *Foreign Affairs*, XXXIV, No. 1. Arthur A. Cohen carries the controversy a step further with the publication of his essay "How Original is Maoism?" *Problems of Communism*, X, No. 6, and his book *The Communism of Mao Tse-tung* (Chicago, 1964), while Stuart R. Schram expresses his views on this problem— which practically settle it—in his paper "On the Nature of Mao Tse-tung's 'Deviation' in 1927," in the *China Quarterly*, No. 18. Intellectually and politically, this insignificant issue has produced a significant result—a better understanding and assessment of Mao as a Marxist-Leninist, especially in the philosophical sense. In this respect, Karl A. Wittfogel's "Some Remarks on Mao's Handling of Concepts and Problems of

Dialectics," *Studies in Soviet Thought*, III (December 4, 1963), is an admirable study. The interest it has aroused is shown in Dennis J. Doolin and Peter J. Golas, *"On Contradiction in the Light of Mao Tse-tung's Essay on 'Dialectical Material-ism,' "* the *China Quarterly*, No. 19, and John E. Rue, "Is Mao Tse-tung's 'Dialectical Materialism' a Forgery?" *Journal of Asian Studies*, XXVI, No. 3. Relevant to this issue is Stuart R. Schram's "Chinese and Leninist Components in the Person-ality of Mao Tse-tung," *Asian Survey*, III, No. 6.

On Mao's military thinking, there are John Gittings, *The Role of the Chinese Army* (London, 1967); Samuel B. Griffith II, *Mao Tse-tung on Guerrilla Warfare*, a translation of an early text by Mao with an introduction (New York, 1961) and his *The Chinese People's Liberation Army* (London, 1968); and Stuart R. Schram's translation of yet another early text by Mao, *Basic Tactics* (New York, 1966). For a general bibli-ographical guide, students are recommended to use Edward J. M. Rhoads, *The Chinese Red Army, 1927–1963: An Anno-tated Bibliography* (Cambridge, Mass., 1964).

The mass line is crucial to an understanding of Mao's po-litical thought and action. Here Stuart R. Schram, *The Po-litical Thought of Mao Tse-tung* (New York, 1963) is an excel-lent study of texts, and James Townsend, *Political Participa-tion in Communist China* (Berkeley, Calif., 1967) is valuable in its analysis of structure and action. The actual process of "persuasion" is analysed in Robert J. Lifton's *Thought Re-form and the Psychology of Totalism: A Study of "Brainwash-ing" in China* (New York, 1961).

Mao's deviations from Marxism-Leninism, in thought as well as in action, are partly responsible for the differences be-tween China and other Communist countries. The historical roots of the differences are traced by Allen S. Whiting, *Soviet Policies in China 1917–1924* (Stanford, Calif., 1953), by Rob-ert C. North, *Moscow and the Chinese Communists* (Stan-ford, Calif., 1953), and by Conrad Brandt, *Stalin's Failure in China* (Cambridge, Mass., 1958). These old roots and new issues grew into the present rift between China and Russia, which is ably handled by Donald S. Zagoria, *The Sino-Soviet Conflict, 1956–1961* (New York, 1964) and by W. E. Griffith, *The Sino-Soviet Rift* (Cambridge, Mass., 1963) and *Sino-Soviet Relations 1964–1965, analysis and documentation* (Cambridge, Mass., 1967).

A highly perceptive analysis by Benjamin Schwartz—"Modernization and the Maoist Vision," *China Quarterly*, No. 21— provides a "lead-in" to the Cultural Revolution, and the pamphlets published by the Foreign Language Press (Peking) in 1967 and 1968, now ten in all, under the title *The Great Socialist Cultural Revolution in China* present the Maoist version of the movement. It is too early to expect a definitive study on this topical subject, but helpful guidance toward an objective understanding may be found in Philip Bridgham, "Mao's 'Cultural Revolution': Origin and Development," in the *China Quarterly*, No. 29 and its sequel in No. 30, and in Charles Neuhauser, "The Great Proletarian Cultural Revolution," in the *China Quarterly*, No. 32. Jack Gray and Patrick Cavendish, *Chinese Communism in Crisis* (London, 1968) is the first monographic treatment of the Cultural Revolution that has the merit of being succinct, clear, and objective, but it suffers from narrow documentation and unevenness.

On Mao's role as a literary figure, there are Michael Bullock and my translations of 37 poems by Mao in *Mao and the Chinese Revolution*, already mentioned, and there are my translation and notes on an unpublished poem by Mao in the *China Quarterly*, No. 34. Stuart R. Schram has also translated and analyzed some of Mao's poems in his essay "Mao as a Poet," in *Problems of Communism*, September–October, 1964. Other discussions on Mao's literary writings are in Cyril Birch, *Chinese Communist Literature* (London, 1963).

There are two minor studies on this great revolutionary— Stuart R. Schram, "Mao Tse-tung and the Secret Societies," and Roxane Witke, "Mao Tse-tung, Women and Suicide in the May Fourth Era," in the *China Quarterly*, Nos. 27 and 31, respectively.

To sum up this brief note, I would like to mention the

symposium "What is Maoism?" in *Problems of Communism*
(September–October, 1966), and a rather pessimistic forecast
by A. Doak Barnett, *China after Mao,* published by Princeton
University Press in 1967.

# Index

**175**

# GREAT LIVES OBSERVED

Gerald Emanuel Stearn, *General Editor*

Other volumes in the series:

# DATE DUE